The Ethics of Health Care Rationing

Should organ transplants be given to patients who have waited the longest, or need it most urgently, or those whose survival prospects are the best? The rationing of health care is universal and inevitable, taking place in poor and affluent countries, in publicly funded and private health care systems. Someone must budget for as well as dispense health care whilst aging populations severely stretch the availability of resources.

The Ethics of Health Care Rationing is a clear and much-needed introduction to this increasingly important topic, considering and assessing the major ethical problems and dilemmas about the allocation, scarcity and rationing of health care. Beginning with a helpful overview of why rationing is an ethical problem, the authors examine the following key topics:

- What is the value of health? How can it be measured?
- What does it mean that a treatment is "good value for money"?
- What sort of distributive principles – utilitarian, egalitarian or prioritarian – should we rely on when thinking about health care rationing?
- Does rationing health care unfairly discriminate against the elderly and people with disabilities?
- Should patients be held responsible for their health? Why does the debate on responsibility for health lead to issues about socioeconomic status and social inequality?

Throughout the book, examples from the US, UK and other countries are used to illustrate the ethical issues at stake. Additional features such as chapter summaries, annotated further reading and discussion questions make this an ideal starting point for students new to the subject, not only in philosophy but also in closely related fields such as politics, health economics, public health, medicine, nursing and social work.

Greg Bognar is Lecturer in Philosophy at the Department of Politics, Philosophy, and Legal Studies, La Trobe University, Australia.

Iwao Hirose is Associate Professor at the Philosophy Department and the School of Environment, McGill University, Canada. He is the author of *Egalitarianism* (2014) and *Moral Aggregation* (2014), and a co-editor of *The Oxford Handbook of Value Theory* (2014) and *Weighing and Reasoning* (2014).

The Ethics of Health Care Rationing

An Introduction

Greg Bognar and Iwao Hirose

Routledge
Taylor & Francis Group

LONDON AND NEW YORK

First published 2014
by Routledge
2 Park Square, Milton Park, Abingdon, Oxon OX14 4RN

and by Routledge
711 Third Avenue, New York, NY 10017

Routledge is an imprint of the Taylor & Francis Group, an informa business

British Library Cataloguing in Publication Data
A catalogue record for this book is available from the British Library

Library of Congress Cataloging in Publication Data
Bognar, Greg.
The ethics of health care rationing : an introduction / Greg Bognar, Iwao Hirose.
Includes bibliographical references and index.
1. Health care rationing–Moral and ethical aspects. I. Hirose, Iwao. II. Title.
RA410.5.B65 2014
174.2–dc23
2013042473

ISBN13: 978-0-415-52115-4 (hbk)
ISBN13: 978-0-415-52118-5 (pbk)
ISBN13: 978-1-315-77824-2 (ebk)

Typeset in Garamond and Gill Sans
by Taylor and Francis Books

To Dan W. Brock

Contents

Acknowledgements   x

Introduction   1

1   Ethics and health care   7

1.1   The vaccination programs   7

1.2   The ubiquity of rationing health care   10

1.3   The inevitability of rationing health care   14

1.4   Moral argument   19

    Chapter summary   25

    Further readings   28

2   The value of health   29

2.1   Well-being and health   29

2.2   Health-related quality of life   33

2.3   Quality-adjusted measures   41

2.4   The burden of disease   43

2.5   Whom to ask?   49

    Chapter summary   51

    Further readings   52

3   Ethics and cost-effectiveness   53

3.1   What is cost-effectiveness analysis?   53

3.2   Calculating health benefits   56

3.3   How is cost-effectiveness analysis used?   59

3.4   Equity weights   66

3.5   Discounting   74

       Chapter summary   77

       Discussion questions   77

       Further readings   78

4   Problems of discrimination   79

4.1   Two lines of attack   79

4.2   Disability discrimination   80

4.3   Fair innings   88

4.4   Age-weighting and the burden of disease   95

4.5   Further moral considerations   98

       Chapter summary   101

       Discussion questions   102

       Further readings   102

5   The aggregation of health benefits   104

5.1   The aggregation problem   104

5.2   The number problem   108

5.3   Fair chances   112

5.4   Choosing patients   116

5.5   Giving priority to the worse off   118

       Chapter summary   124

       Discussion questions   125

       Further readings   125

6   Responsibility for health   127

6.1   Equality and luck   127

6.2   An alternative proposal   134

6.3   Are smokers really responsible?   139

6.4   The social gradient in health   141

6.5   Social justice and health care rationing   145

Chapter summary   149

Discussion questions   149

Further readings   150

Conclusion   **151**

Glossary   *158*
Bibliography   *161*
Index   *167*

Acknowledgements

This book project grew out of our discussions and collaborative research over many years. We first learned about the issues in this book while we were Post-Doctoral Research Fellows at the Harvard University Program in Ethics and Health. We thank Dan W. Brock, Norman Daniels, and Daniel Wikler at the Program for their guidance and encouragement over the years. In addition, we thank Daniel Wikler for permission to use the vaccination program example that we describe in Chapter 1.

Many people sent us written comments on earlier versions of the draft. We learned a great deal from these comments, even if we could not always do justice to them in the final version. We also had to leave out several suggestions for including additional topics simply because of space constraints. With these caveats, we thank Yukiko Asada, Rob Baltussen, Kristine Bærøe, Dan Hausman, Samuel J. Kerstein, Ingrid Miljeteig, Erik Nord, Ole Frithjof Norheim, and three anonymous reviewers for Routledge. Many more people helped us with their questions in conversation and at public lectures. We thank audiences at Charles Sturt University, the Eindhoven University of Technology, the Fondation Brocher, Georgia State University, the Program in Ethics & Health at Harvard University, La Trobe University, Monash University, the Blavatnik School of Government at the University of Oxford, the Universidad Nacional Autonoma de Mexico, University of Bergen, University of Connecticut at Storrs, University of Leeds, University of Melbourne, the Conference on Distributive Justice in Health at the Centre for Humanistic Studies of the University of Minho, and the Ethics Center at the University of Zurich.

We would also like to thank our students who served as guinea pigs for this material. Their feedback has improved the book in many ways. In the fall semester of 2012, Hirose taught the material in this book for undergraduates at McGill University, and Bognar taught it at La Trobe University. Bognar also taught some of the material in the book at the "Justice: Theory and Applications" summer university program of the Central European University in 2013.

We want to express our special gratitude to Fondation Brocher. The Brocher Visiting Fellowship enabled Hirose to complete Chapters 5 and 6 in a beautiful research environment in spring 2012, and the 2012 Brocher Summer Academy brought Bognar to the Villa Brocher for three days of discussion and joint revision of the first complete draft.

Hirose gratefully acknowledges the financial support from the Canadian Institutes of Health Research. Bognar thanks the journal *Bioethics* for its permission to use material from his article, "Fair Innings" (forthcoming).

Despite some disagreements about other philosophical issues, we have no disagreement about what is presented in this book. Bognar is primarily responsible for Chapters 2 through 4, and Hirose for Chapters 5 and 6. Bognar and Hirose are jointly responsible for the Introduction, Chapter 1, and the Conclusion.

Last, but not least, we thank our editors at Routledge, Tony Bruce and Adam Johnson, for their support of this project.

Introduction

Rationing health care, we suspect, sounds like a horrible idea. For some, the word *rationing* conjures up images of wartime hardships – long lines waiting at distribution points for basic necessities such as bread, sugar, cooking oil, or gasoline. For others, health care rationing sounds like the government intruding on people's private lives with its bureaucrats lording over life and death, deciding whether Grandma can get her medicines or the life-saving treatment she needs. In some countries, the idea of rationing raises fears about privatizing cherished universal health care systems, destroying social solidarity and reducing people to commodities.

Rationing, in its broadest sense, is the controlled allocation of some scarce resource or good. It implies that limits are placed on its availability. People who need or want the rationed good are restricted to getting it in a certain quantity or size or at a certain time. They are not free to use or consume it in the way they want.

In health care, rationing can apply to treatments, services, pharmaceuticals, medical procedures, and so on. When health care resources are rationed, patients may be restricted to certain treatments. They might be placed on waiting lists. There might be limits on how often they are eligible for diagnostic procedures or screening tests. And, in the worst case, patients may be denied beneficial or even life-saving treatments and interventions. No doubt many people feel that rationing health care is not just a nuisance – it can seriously affect quality of life, and it might even, literally, be a matter of life and death.

When health care is rationed, then somewhere, someone made a decision about the limits of what is provided or how it is provided. For instance, someone decided that hospitals cannot perform a particular kind of surgery. Someone decided a particular type of medicine is not subsidized. Someone organized patients into a waiting list. As we will say, someone made a *priority setting* decision, choosing which beneficial treatments or interventions are more important than others, which have the best value, which are not important at all. All of these decisions interfere with our freedom to decide, together with our doctors, what sort of intervention, or treatment, or medicine, or medical technology we need or want. All of them interfere with our freedom as patients and health care consumers. They are choices that are imposed on us. The priorities of those who made the decisions may often conflict with our own priorities.

So, if rationing health care is a horrible idea, the *ethics* of rationing health care is even worse. It sounds like an oxymoron. If rationing health care is horrible, how can it be ethical?

Our aim in this book is to show you that health care rationing not only *can* be ethical, but it *must* be. Our case is very simple. We shall argue that the rationing of health care resources is inevitable. It takes place in all health care systems – public or private, rich or poor. It is not only inevitable, it is actually ubiquitous. So you might consider it a necessary evil. But then it is crucial that it is done as ethically as possible to reduce its evil. Hence you should care about the ethics of rationing health care. It is not an oxymoron.

Actually, we will also make a stronger argument. We will argue that rationing in health care is not only inevitable and widespread, but it is also *desirable*. Health care rationing, or setting priorities between alternative resource uses, is far from a necessary evil – it is a good thing. We all benefit when health care resources are allocated in a morally defensible way. This is another reason why you should care about the ethics of rationing health care.

To many people, these claims may sound incredible. They associate health care rationing with poor countries. It is not something, they believe, that takes place – or should take place – in affluent countries. But the truth is, the health care systems of the most developed countries do ration health care one way or another. As a matter of fact, the careful rationing of health care is one of the factors that make a health care system work well. The best health care systems in the world do it.

Other people associate health care rationing with governments. It is, they believe, something that takes place only in single-payer, government-run health care systems. Some people who have this belief probably have private health insurance. So they believe they are not affected by rationing.

The truth is, privately run health care is rationed just as much as publicly run health care. The rationing is done by the companies providing health insurance. They might offer a choice between different plans, but they all involve limits and controls on what they offer. Rationing is not confined to governments only.

When we were planning this book, many people advised us against using the word *rationing*. They worried about its negative, and often political, connotations. Some philosophers have recently stopped using the "R-word" altogether. We believe this is a mistake. It's a perfectly accurate word for the subject. It should not be yielded to those who attempt to use it to raise public fears for their own political gain. It should be defended. Health care is too important to allow the muddying of the waters by a fear to call things by their names.

Our central claim is that the rationing of health care is an ethical problem. Setting priorities in health care must be based on sound moral principles. This book provides an introduction to this complex topic. While there are excellent books on health care rationing in philosophy, health economics, and health policy, they tend to be written with a specialist audience in mind. We are unaware of any other entry-level book. In fact, our topic has, until recently, received little attention in ethics.

The area of philosophy that is closest to our concerns is bioethics. Traditionally, bioethics has focused on ethical issues that arise in the doctor–patient relationship and in medical research. It has addressed topics such as the permissibility of abortion or physician-assisted suicide, embryonic stem-cell research, respect for patient autonomy, or the protection of research subjects. More recently, as health care has become an important focus of public debate all around the world, some bioethicists have started to address questions that arise at the population level – for instance, questions about increasing international and domestic inequalities in health, the health-related causes and consequences of poverty, the aging of societies, and the allocation of health care resources. This relatively new area of philosophy has become known as *population-level bioethics*. We have learned a lot from people working in this area, and we point the reader to their works at the end of each chapter in the *Further Readings* section.

The problem of health care rationing is complex. For one thing, most examples of rationing in health care are rather mundane, uncontroversial, even boring. They concern setting levels of subsidies for pharmaceuticals, levels of co-payments for health care services, reimbursement policies for medical devices, and similar decisions within complex administrative institutions. They do not make for striking examples. The examples that are usually employed in discussions of rationing are more fascinating, but also more unusual, and hence less representative. They concern expensive cancer drugs that provide a few months of remission at enormous costs, patients on waiting lists for scarce transplantable organs, or priority lists for vaccinations during an influenza pandemic. We ourselves will use such examples in this book. But it is important to keep in mind that most examples of health care rationing are much more pedestrian.

In addition, health care institutions differ from country to country. To keep our discussion concise, we ignore many of these differences. Our aim is to highlight the general ethical questions and moral principles that apply equally to different settings and health care systems. We focus on the general issues that any attempt of priority setting must face. For instance, we do not have anything to say about whether a health care system should be run publicly or rely on private health insurance, or how taxpayers and patients should share the costs of health care. But the questions we do raise are relevant to various institutional arrangements. Our hope is to furnish readers with a clear understanding of at least the basics of the complex problems surrounding the ethics of health care rationing.

Still, there are many questions and ideas that we have to address in this book. Before we embark on the journey, it is worth having a road map in our hands.

We will begin in the next chapter by defending the two claims that we have already made. We show why health care rationing is widespread and explain why it is also inevitable. The explanation has to do with the unavoidability of scarcity. We present some general ways in which scarcity arises in health care. In later chapters, we will give more specific real-life examples of resource scarcity and the way rationing can address it. Before that, we also give a very brief introduction to moral argument and explain some central ethical concepts and ideas. This will provide the necessary background for later discussions.

If the rationing of health care resources is inevitable, then we must be able to compare different resource allocations as better or worse, acceptable or unacceptable, and so on. Since the goods and resources that are allocated in health care are diverse, we need common criteria for their evaluation. Chapter 2 addresses this issue. Naturally, you might think, a common criterion should be health: one way of allocating resources is better than another if it results in better health for people. But health is not a quantity that can be measured, like weight or height. Its measurement consists in considering its value, through its impact on quality of life. We explain how researchers try to measure the value of health by examining the quality of life judgments that people make about the badness of health states. These judgments can help compare alternative allocations. But measuring the value of health is riddled with problems and puzzles. We present some of these problems and puzzles in connection with two of the most widespread measures of the value of health: quality-adjusted life years (QALYs) and disability-adjusted life years (DALYs).

For readers new to our topic, Chapter 2 is probably going to be the most tedious in this book. We apologize for that. Nevertheless, it introduces concepts and ideas without which the material in subsequent chapters would be much more difficult to understand.

Chapter 3 is about cost-effectiveness analysis. This is the policymaker's main tool for evaluating the costs and benefits of different interventions and health care services. But the use of cost-effectiveness analysis for setting priorities among different uses of health care resources is controversial – not only among academics and policymakers, but also among the general public. In this chapter, we explain how cost-effectiveness analysis works, address the main ethical problems of its use, and correct some misunderstandings that often appear in discussions. We also present several examples.

Chapter 4 addresses two problems for cost-effectiveness analysis. One of these problems is discrimination against people with disabilities and chronic health conditions. Some people believe that if health care resource allocation is based on a principle that directs you to maximize health benefits, you will often give priority to people without disabilities, and the health care needs of people with disabilities will be neglected. We show that this worry is based on misunderstandings. But the objection does raise some important issues about moral considerations that would be ignored if we focused only on costs and benefits.

The second problem is discrimination by age. Some people believe that age should be a relevant consideration in the allocation of health care resources. In particular, the health needs of younger people should have higher priority than the health needs of the elderly. We try to provide a coherent formulation of this view, but we ultimately leave the question of age discrimination open. People have different moral intuitions about particular cases, and controversies about the role of age and disability in resource allocation have arisen in many practical applications. With aging societies and the ever-growing prevalence of chronic illness, these controversies are going to become more and more acute. We close this chapter by discussing further moral considerations that could be used in conjunction with cost-effectiveness analysis.

Chapter 5 broadens the discussion by connecting the problem of health care rationing to more general debates in ethical theory. This is the chapter in which you encounter striking, imagined and real-life examples of deciding who should live and who should die. Our aim is to show how some of the moral principles used in health care resource allocation lead to familiar, but deeply controversial, problems in ethical theory. These problems concern the aggregation of benefits across different people, the moral justification of taking into account the number of those who benefit, and the use of lotteries in life-and-death cases.

The last full chapter broadens the discussion even further. It begins by focusing on a controversial issue in public health: should individual responsibility for health and healthy lifestyles be taken into account in the provision of health services and treatment decisions? Some influential theories in political philosophy hold that inequalities are not a matter of justice if they are the result of choices for which individuals can be held responsible. It is not unjust if some people end up with disadvantages through their own choice or fault. Society, as a matter of justice, is not required to come to their aid to reduce their disadvantages.

The theme of individual responsibility is becoming more and more prevalent in public debates. The application of some theories of distributive justice to health care seems to suggest that individual responsibility should have a central role in health care rationing. But very few authors have brought together the philosophical and the practical arguments on this topic. We will connect the two debates. We will also emphasize that the question of responsibility quickly leads to broader issues about the relation between health and behavior, class, race, and socioeconomic status. We give a very brief account of the growing literature on the social determinants of health that examines these issues.

In the Conclusion, we return to a claim we made a few pages back: that the rationing of health care is not only inevitable and widespread, but it is both morally defensible and desirable. It is a good thing from which we all benefit. Of course, this is the case only if rationing choices are based on sound ethical principles and made transparently and accountably. We conclude by defending this idea.

The arguments and ideas in the following chapters are sometimes complex and might require some patience on the part of the reader. We have attempted to present them as clearly as possible. We do not assume any prior knowledge of philosophy, health economics, medicine, or health policy. At times, we use numerical examples. They never rely on anything beyond the most basic math skills. For those who want to explore the topics in greater depth, each chapter ends with a list of further readings and discussion questions.

I Ethics and health care

1.1 The vaccination programs

Imagine that you and your team of public health experts are contracted by the government of a remote, tiny island state to vaccinate children against a fatal disease. The disease threatens only children, and each child has an equal chance of contracting it. The vaccination has no side effects and provides total immunity against the disease.

Altogether, there are 1,000 children on the island. Eight hundred of them live on the coastal plains and 200 live in remote mountains. It costs only $1 to vaccinate a child who lives near the coast, but $4 to vaccinate a child who lives in the mountains. It costs four times as much to vaccinate the children in the mountains because it is difficult to reach them.

The problem is that you are only given $800 for this work (this is a very poor country). You and your team cannot vaccinate all the children. Because of logistical reasons, you have to choose between two ways of organizing your vaccination campaign. The two programs are:

(A) vaccinating every child living on the coastal plains, but none of the children living in the mountains;
(B) vaccinating half of the children who live on the coastal plains, and half of those who live in the mountains.

Which program would you choose?

If you choose Program A, 800 children will be vaccinated. They will be protected against the disease. If you choose Program B, half of the children on the plains and half of the children in the mountains will be selected randomly. In the end, 500 children will be vaccinated – 400 on the plains and 100 in the mountains.

We often present this example to our students. We ask them to make a choice between these hypothetical programs. We get very consistent results. A majority of the students in any class chooses Program A, but there is always a fairly large minority that chooses Program B. Students disagree about the right choice. We have never met a class where there was anything approaching consensus in favor of either program.

Next, we ask a follow-up question from those who are in favor of Program A.

Here is the question. Suppose that just as you are about to leave the island with your team, you get a call from the Ministry of Health. They are happy to tell you that the government has given you another $800 for a second round of vaccinations. Even better, they also have vaccinations available against a second disease. This disease is just like the first: it only affects children, it is invariably fatal, all children have the same chance of contracting it, and anyone's chance of contracting it is equal to the chance of contracting the first disease.

At this point, you have a meeting with your team to discuss your options. For logistical reasons, you must choose between the following two programs:

(C) vaccinating all the children who live in the mountains against the first disease;
(D) vaccinating all the children who live on the coastal plains against the second disease.

If you choose Program C, you will vaccinate all the 1,000 children living on the island against the first disease. If you choose Program D, you will vaccinate 800 children against both diseases. In the first case, you will provide 1,000 vaccinations to 1,000 children; in the second case, you will provide 1,600 vaccinations to 800 children.

Would you choose Program C or Program D?

In our experience, an overwhelming majority of the students who favored Program A chooses Program C. We have met very few students who favor A *and* D.

Those who favor Program A in the first question usually give the following explanation for their choice. The vaccination confers a great benefit – immunity against a fatal disease. It is very important to provide this benefit to as many children as possible. Of course, Program A leaves out the children who live in the mountains. But for each child that you could vaccinate in the mountains, you can vaccinate four children on the plains. Choosing Program A is justified by the benefits that would be bestowed on a greater number of children.

Those who favor Program B have a different explanation. They argue that it is wrong to exclude the children living in the mountains. It is not their fault that they live in a remote place. There is something unfair about discriminating against some of the children merely because they are growing up in less accessible places. If not all of the children can be vaccinated, you should at least give an equal chance to all of those who live on the coastal plains and all of those who live in the mountains. To these students, this seems to be a requirement of fairness.

Remarkably, those who choose A *and* C tend to give a similar explanation for choosing Program C in the second question. For these students, maximizing the benefits of vaccination is the most important consideration in the first question. But the consideration of fairness appears in the second question and becomes more important than benefit maximization – even if very few students might be able to explain what precisely they mean by fairness.

At this point, those who favored Program B – vaccinating half of the children on the plains and half of the children in the mountains – also get a second question. Here is their question. Just as you are preparing to leave the island, you get a call from the Ministry of Health. You are given another $800 for vaccinations. You and your team have to decide between two programs:

(E) vaccinating the remaining half of the children who live on the coastal plains and the remaining half of those who live in the mountains;
(F) vaccinating all the children who live on the coastal plains against the second disease.

If you choose Program E, you will end up vaccinating all the 1,000 children living on the island against the first disease. You will end up giving out 1,000 vaccinations to 1,000 children. If you choose Program F, you will end up vaccinating one half of the children on the plains against both diseases, the other half of the children on the plains against the second disease only, and one half of the children in the mountains only against the first disease. Altogether, you end up providing 1,300 vaccinations (800 + 400 + 100) to 900 children.

Which program would you choose?

In our experience, a large majority of those who favored Program B in the first question favors Program F in the second question – even if there are typically some holdouts favoring B and E. Program F usually gets a comfortable majority. When asked to explain their choices, students often say that although they continue to believe that it is important to avoid the unfairness of choosing Program A in the first question, they acknowledge that the greater benefits of Program F can tilt the balance in the second question. After all, if you implement programs B and F, you will vaccinate nine tenths of the children against at least one disease, and a significant minority against two.

When we present these questions, we emphasize that we are not looking for "right" or "wrong" answers. Rather, what matters is what we can learn from the answers about our moral beliefs. And the lesson is clear: most people who consider this example believe that it is important to choose the course of action that will bring about the greatest benefits – but they also believe that it is important to allocate resources in a "fair" way. Of course, we need to say a lot more about the requirement of fairness. But one thing is already clear: fairness and benefit maximization can, and often do, conflict. It is important to find the right balance between them. This book is about how we can do that.

1.2 The ubiquity of rationing health care

The story of the vaccination programs is a thought experiment. By asking you to make moral judgments in hypothetical situations, it is designed to shed light on the ethical principles that are relevant to the distribution of benefits in conditions when resources are scarce. Philosophers often use thought experiments to help analyze difficult questions. They often involve an element of science fiction: you are asked to imagine that you are a brain in a vat, or you are teleported to another planet, or you are deceived by an evil demon. But the vaccination story is different. It is not entirely fictional. It is modeled on a real-life ethical dilemma.

In 2003, the World Health Organization (WHO) and the Joint United Nations Programme on HIV and AIDS (UNAIDS) launched the "3 by 5" program. The aim of the program was to provide antiretroviral therapy to three million people with HIV/AIDS living in developing countries before the end of 2005. Even if successful, the program would have reached only a fraction of those who could have benefited from the therapy. In the end, the target was met only in 2007. At the end of 2011, around 6.65 million eligible patients in developing countries received antiretroviral therapy, up from 400,000 in 2003. But still less than half of eligible patients had access to therapy.

One controversial aspect of rolling out the program was whether delivery should focus on urban or rural populations. In developing countries, there is a shortage of HIV clinics and health facilities. Concentrating delivery in urban areas ensured that more patients could be reached, but it made the program inaccessible to rural populations. Patients living far from cities could not reach the facilities because of long distances, bad roads, and their inability to pay for transport. Some experts argued that the program should focus on those areas where the infrastructure is already in place, in order to reach as many people as quickly as possible. Others argued that rural populations should not be neglected, even if fewer patients can be served as a consequence.

Thus, policymakers faced the same dilemma as our students in the classroom. The choices they made, however, had real consequences. For some people, they were a matter of life and death. But national guidelines for implementing the program often treated such dilemmas as merely technical questions: matters that require the expertise of medical doctors, economists, and policymakers. The ethical nature of the dilemmas was rarely acknowledged, and the choices were made without consulting the citizens of these countries.

It is understandable that hard ethical choices are sometimes treated as technical questions. The policymakers who were responsible for broadening access to antiretroviral therapy had to set priorities among competing resource uses. They had to engage in the rationing of health care. But the idea of rationing health care makes people uncomfortable. It entails that there are patients who could benefit from care but have to do without it. Many people get upset when they hear or read stories in which someone is denied potentially beneficial (maybe even life-saving) medical care. In many countries, the very idea of rationing health care is taboo. Politicians who talk about it risk their prospects for reelection. So it is not surprising that rationing choices are often hidden behind technical or medical language.

Still, it is not right. It is the responsibility of policymakers to reflect on the values they take into account when they make choices about the use of social resources – both in health care and beyond. It is our right as citizens to demand that social choices that can potentially have a great effect on our lives are made in a transparent and accountable manner. It is also our responsibility to think through the ethical issues faced by our society. We should have the chance to contribute to their discussion and resolution. To do that, we need a basic understanding of medical and economic matters; but what we need most is ethical argument. Medical doctors and economists can help us understand technical matters, and philosophers can help us with the ethical argument.

So, the first point we want to make is that the rationing of health care is an ethical issue. We all have a stake in getting it right. Next, we want to argue that health care rationing is ubiquitous. It affects all of us.

Some readers might think that the rationing of health care has little to do with their society. Where they live, there is a well-functioning health care system. They might think that rationing is something that takes place mainly in resource-poor environments or the least developed countries. True, the "3 by 5" program targeted middle- and low-income countries. But it would be a mistake to conclude from this one example that only these countries should be concerned with rationing. In fact, rationing is universal. It takes place in poor as well as affluent countries, in publicly funded health care systems as well as in private health insurance.

Other readers might associate the rationing of health care with government – in particular, with faceless bureaucrats in drab offices making life-and-death choices. In the vaccination program, you probably assumed that you were working for the government or perhaps an NGO (non-governmental organization). But you would have faced the very same choices if you were a private contractor with expertise in public health campaigns. The need to set priorities in health care is not limited to government-run health care systems. Private actors, including insurance providers, need to do it just as much.

Neither is it the case that rationing is an exception in affluent countries, rather than the rule. Most people in affluent countries could probably mention organ transplantation as an example of health care rationing. Because there are many more patients than available organs, patients everywhere are placed on waiting lists. Tragically, some of them die before a suitable donor is found. Waiting lists are a form of rationing. It is not difficult to see how they raise ethical issues. Should priority be given to the patients who have waited the longest, or to those who need an organ most urgently, or to those whose survival prospects are the best? Clearly, these are partly ethical, rather than merely medical questions.

Similarly, many readers might recall the worries about pandemic flu. Because of the fear of a worldwide avian or swine flu pandemic, governments are trying to develop and stockpile vaccines. However, if a new type of virus appears, it might take several months before a vaccine can be developed and produced in sufficient quantities. In the meantime, it will be necessary to set priorities among different patient groups. Who should be vaccinated first? Should it be the young or the old? Those who are already sick, or those who are particularly vulnerable? Is it fair to give priority to those who have dependents? Many governments have drawn up contingency plans for a pandemic. In these plans, they have to answer these questions. Clearly, these are partly ethical, rather than merely technical questions.

These examples are familiar. But they are also the most unusual. They concern extreme cases of scarcity and public health emergencies. In such cases, rationing might be unavoidable. But what about our claim that health care rationing is ubiquitous?

In a way, what is rationed in these examples are people. Patients are matched to resources. The examples present choices about who gets medical treatment or who gets it before others. They make good topics for debate, but they are far from ordinary. Most rationing choices are not like this. They do not concern setting priorities among patients. They concern setting priorities among treatments, services, pharmaceuticals, medical procedures, and so on. They concern *what* to provide in the health care system and how to provide it, not to whom to provide it.

Health care rationing is the controlled allocation of scarce health care resources. Occasionally it takes the form of selecting particular patients or patient groups. But usually it takes the form of setting priorities among interventions. By "intervention," we mean any use of resources in the health care system that aims to address health problems and risks of health problems. By "resource use," we mean any mobilization of human, physical, financial, or other sorts of assets to achieve these aims.

Thus, when the government decides which pharmaceuticals to subsidize from the health care budget, it engages in rationing. When it decides in which city to build a hospital or clinic, it is an example of rationing. When it introduces a cancer-screening program, it is rationing health care. All of these decisions require resources that could be spent elsewhere. Implicitly or indirectly, all such decisions determine who will benefit. Patients of subsidized medicines have to spend less than others. Residents of the city in which the hospital is built have better access to specialist services.

Private health insurance is no different. When an insurance provider decides which treatments to include in its plans, it engages in rationing. When it determines the co-payments, its choice is an example of rationing. When it refuses to provide coverage for people with preexisting conditions, it is, obviously, rationing health care by excluding these people.

Most of us experience the consequences of rationing at some point in our life. When a doctor prescribes a medicine for you that is not subsidized by the health care system or your insurance provider, you might be facing the consequences of a rationing decision that was made by others. When you are told that you need a procedure but it will take many months before you can get it, it might be because of choices made about the use of health care resources. You have to wait because resources are scarce and hence their allocation is controlled. Perhaps the procedures are scheduled on the "first-come, first-served" basis. This in itself is a form of rationing. The procedures could be scheduled on some other basis.

Most of us are unaware that rationing decisions take place all the time because of the enormous complexity of modern health care systems. Rationing is almost never a matter of simple choices between this or that intervention. Rather, it is a matter of trying to achieve different (and often conflicting) objectives, of making trade-offs between different resource uses, of trying to create as much benefit as possible from limited resources. When we are faced with the consequences of rationing decisions, the consequences are often indirect and sometimes unintended. Indeed, it is not easy to find simple real-life examples of health care rationing. But that is because real-life examples are complex, not because they are rare.

It would be a mistake to think that rationing decisions are intended to make your life harder, or to deny you benefits to which you should be entitled. On the contrary, the rationing of health care ought to serve the purpose of benefiting everyone. But not everyone can be benefited all the time. Your medicine might not be subsidized because it provides little benefits to patients, and it is better to spend the money on medicines that provide more significant benefits. But you are more likely to take notice when you have to pay the full costs, and less likely to take notice when you benefit from not having to pay the full costs. You will not be thinking on these occasions about the benefits of health care rationing. If health care resources are allocated fairly and efficiently, everyone benefits. But people take the benefits for granted.

This is why the ethics of health care rationing is so important. If health care resources are allocated unfairly and inefficiently, many people will fail to receive benefits that they should, and could, get. This is morally wrong. But even when the allocation of health care resources is fair and efficient, there must be limits on what can be provided. Some patients will be disadvantaged by these limits. Thus, the limits must be morally justified. Otherwise, they impose unacceptable burdens on those patients.

Our discussion so far has left one question unaddressed: Why is rationing in health care inevitable? The answer is *scarcity*. Health care resources are scarce. This is why we must set priorities. But this answer just leads to another question: Why are health care resources scarce? Why can't we simply spend more on health care so that there is no need for rationing resources?

1.3 The inevitability of rationing health care

There are many reasons for the scarcity of health care resources. Some of these are technological: in the last few decades, medicine has made enormous advances. It is now possible to cure many previously fatal diseases and to manage long-term chronic conditions. We can now do more than ever before to restore and maintain health. But being able to do more also means spending more. The expansion of health services accounts for most of the increase in health care spending that has taken place over the last 50 years or so. This will continue. Our increasing understanding of genetics, for example, promises to lead to new, and usually more costly therapies. As our armory to fight disease expands, the pressure on health care budgets is going to increase further.

Other reasons are demographic. Life expectancies are increasing almost everywhere. Meanwhile, in many countries fewer children are born. Aging societies spend more on health. Usually, people need health care the most in their very first, and then in their last few years. In developed countries, aging accounts for a substantive share of the increase in health care spending. Since the populations of many developed countries are aging rapidly, we can expect the growth of spending to continue.

There are also economic reasons. It is difficult to design a health care system that works efficiently. As a patient, you usually do not know enough about your condition to decide on the best treatment. The decision needs expert knowledge. Thus, you are not like a consumer looking for something to eat for lunch, who can use her experience and easily available information to make an informed choice. You rely on your doctor to tell you what you need. Moreover, patients often do not directly bear the costs (or all of the costs) of health care services. Since they are less sensitive to costs, they tend to demand more. When it comes to your health, it is better to be sure. An additional diagnostic procedure may just bring you peace of mind, even if, from a medical perspective, it is unlikely to be useful.

At the same time, doctors are often in a difficult situation. They are obligated to give you the best diagnosis and treatment. But they are also expected to act as gatekeepers – making sure that you use only the services that you really need. There can be a tension between their obligations to you as a patient and their role in ensuring that medical resources are used well. It is difficult to find the appropriate balance between these obligations. If doctors, hospitals, or other actors in the health care system are not sensitive to costs, they are more likely to contribute to the misuse and waste of resources. The problem, to put it in the economist's terms, is that incentives are often distorted in the health care system. Controlling costs is difficult.

Overuse of resources can obviously lead to scarcity. But sometimes this can happen in striking ways. In recent years, researchers have raised the alarm that our indiscriminate use of antibiotics might lead to the emergence of resistant strains of bacteria. For instance, there are worries that extensively drug-resistant tuberculosis might lead to an epidemic in the future. If cheap, easily available antibiotics do not work anymore, the health care system has to rely on more costly alternatives. This is harmful for everyone – each dollar that has to be spent on more expensive antibiotic treatments could have been used elsewhere in the health care system. Everyone would benefit if the use of antibiotics was more tightly controlled.

The way health care resources are distributed can itself contribute to scarcity. According to the data available at the time of writing, the United States spent 17.6 percent of its GDP on health care, almost double the average of the OECD countries, a rich-country club. Yet almost 50 million people – over 16 percent of the population – had no health insurance. Worse, the average life expectancy in the US is lower than in many other countries, including some that are much poorer. Americans do not get better health for the extra dollars they spend on health care. This suggests that a lot of their spending is less efficient than it should be.

Our example about the vaccination programs illustrates yet another way that scarcity can arise. Interventions and health care services are seldom sufficiently divisible to ensure equal access. If you are worried about the distribution of income, you can, in principle, redistribute it any way you like (since money can be divided up as finely as you want). But you cannot redistribute health care resources the same way. You cannot build a hospital in every village. Decisions about the location of health care infrastructure and the organization of health care delivery inevitably create inequalities of access, which can itself be a form of scarcity. In the vaccination example and the "3 by 5" program, the costs of reaching some populations increased scarcity.

Hence, scarcity and access are closely related. We can agree that everyone should have access to basic health care services; no one should be excluded from the health care system. But equal access cannot mean access to everything by everyone. Limits must be set, and they inevitably create restrictions on access to particular interventions and services.

Unequal access is problematic for a further reason. People are generally more tolerant of income inequalities than inequalities in health and access to health care services. They believe that inequalities in income and wealth, at least within certain limits, might be beneficial for society: they create incentives or reflect differential effort. But very few people believe that similar considerations apply to health. Health inequalities have no beneficial social effects, and they rarely, if ever, reflect "effort" (an issue to which we will return in Chapter 6). Thus, many people would consider inequalities in health and access to health care much more troubling than other forms of inequality. Even those who do not consider income inequality unfair might be worried about inequalities in health and in the delivery of health care.

For the reasons listed, scarcity is inevitable in health care. Since it is inevitable, rationing is indispensable: societies must try to allocate the available health care resources efficiently and equitably. This is the only way to avoid inefficiency, waste, and unfairness.

Some people want to resist this conclusion. Scarcity in health care, they argue, should not be managed. Instead, it should be eliminated. Since health is important, we should spend more on it. This objection basically says that there is always more money. You just have to find it.

There is an element of truth in this objection. Surely, sometimes the right response to scarcity is to get rid of it. There are still many people in low-income countries who do not get antiretroviral therapy. More should be spent to ensure that they do. Affluent countries could, and arguably should, do much more to help achieve this.

Even so, the objection underestimates the gravity of the problem. Suppose you become a powerful, but benevolent dictator. Since you want to use your power to help people, you decide to eliminate scarcity in health care. You decide to spend enough to keep up with technological developments and scientific breakthroughs. You spend enough to meet every medical need in a rapidly aging society. You manage to eliminate economic inefficiencies and distorted incentives from the health care system. You introduce policies to provide equal access to everyone. Have you overcome the need for rationing?

For several reasons, you have not. First, even if the most apparent forms of scarcity are eliminated, others remain. Even if every potentially beneficial intervention is available, you will still have to decide which to offer first – you cannot offer everything, everywhere, all the time. You will still have to decide whether to organize a cancer-screening program or a maternal health campaign first. Time is a scarce resource. There is only so far you can go to eliminate scarcity by spending more money.

Second, you will soon realize that in health care, resource use and its costs can easily spiral out of hand. Suppose you introduce more successful cancer treatments. Because better treatments are available, more people are screened. Since more people are screened, more cases are found and treated. No doubt, it is better that fewer people die prematurely because of cancer. But screening and treatment have increased your costs exponentially, creating scarcity elsewhere in the health care system. So you have to increase spending further, which may in turn lead to further scarcity. Paradoxically, better health services can increase scarcity.

Third, eliminating scarcity itself requires rationing choices, since the only way you can get rid of scarcity is by setting priorities. You can only avoid inefficiencies if you spend resources the most efficient way. You can only achieve better health outcomes for the whole population if you take into account the benefits and the costs of interventions. You can only reduce health inequalities if you set the right priorities among the needs of different groups within the population. These are all rationing questions.

At the end of the day, your "war on scarcity" is likely to leave you with a depleted budget. At this point, you are faced with the question: Was it worth it? Health care competes with other social goods. When resources are spent on health, there is less for education, for infrastructure projects, for national defense. Sometimes, resources spent on health would do more good elsewhere. Priorities must be set both within health care and between health and other social objectives.

So, no matter where you turn, you face the need for rationing. Even for a benevolent dictator, this must be very annoying.

Some people might object that since health care saves lives, expenditures on health (or at least on life-extending interventions) should have absolute priority. But there are other ways to save lives. Highway safety regulations are a more effective way to do it. Moreover, few people would agree, on reflection, that saving lives should always have priority. Later in the book, we will describe some examples of drugs that can extend the lives of people with terminal cancer for a few weeks or months – at enormous expense. All the money spent on these treatments has to come from somewhere. There is nothing morally objectionable in asking whether these treatments are worth their costs. There might be a point at which saving lives is just not worthwhile any more.

Other people reject the need for rationing for another reason. Health, they argue, is fundamentally important to well-being. Because it is so important, you are entitled to it: you have a right to health. If you have a right to something, then you should be provided with it, and you should be provided with it even when the cost–benefit calculation is unfavorable.

But the idea of a right to health is ambiguous at best. At some point in your life, you will inevitably fall ill. You will die some day. Are your rights violated then? Who violates them? It is better to treat the right to health as a right to *health care*. But this is problematic too. Do you have a right to all sorts of health care, no matter how little the benefits? What about the costs? (Do you have to bear the costs yourself? If you have a right to something, should you bear its costs? What if you cannot afford it?) The right to health care had better not be interpreted as the right to any amount or form of health care. At the most, it should be interpreted as a right to *basic* health care: as the right to fundamentally important forms of health care.

Interpreted this way, this proposal just takes us back to the original issue. You have to decide which interventions and services are "basic" or fundamentally important. Surely, those that have the greatest benefits or prevent the greatest loss in health should belong to this group. Interventions and services that bring little benefit should not. But making this distinction requires you to settle questions of priority. It does not liberate you from the need to face the question of rationing – in fact, it requires it. Treating some forms of health care as a matter of rights does not avoid the problem. It just conceals it.

Scarcity is always present in health care systems. Therefore, rationing is inevitable. If you try to eliminate or minimize scarcity, you have to set priorities. That also requires rationing. You cannot escape it. Since rationing is inevitable, it is all the more important to get it right. Since it is a moral issue, "getting it right" requires thinking carefully through the ethical questions that it raises. This is what the following chapters will help you do.

Before we embark on this project, we need to introduce some general ideas about ethics. How can we settle moral questions? How should ethical argument proceed? What are the main ethical concepts and theories that are relevant to the topic of this book? We will now look at these questions before returning to health in Chapter 2.

1.4 Moral argument

Ethics is the study of right and wrong. It is concerned with developing and defending principles and theories that can be used to determine which acts or policies are right and which are wrong. It helps us decide which moral judgments to accept and which to reject. In everyday life, all of us make moral judgments. We say it is wrong to tell a lie; it is wrong to bully classmates; it is right to give up your seat on the bus to an elderly person. Rightness and wrongness are normative properties of action. Telling a lie is to make a false claim to someone with the intention of deceiving them. Instances of telling a lie have the property of wrongness. It is a normative property, because it concerns the value of the act, or what ought to be done. (Perhaps telling a lie can be justified in some circumstances. But even then, it has this property. It is just that other considerations count for more in the balance of reasons.)

Ethics is interested in the normative properties that make acts or policies right or wrong. (Some professional philosophers distinguish ethics and morality. But we will use these two words interchangeably throughout this book.)

Some types of acts are right. Some types of acts are wrong. Ethical theories aim to provide a coherent framework for determining their rightness and wrongness, and to govern the conduct of a person or collective body. Moral principles apply to everyone – even those who do not accept them. That is, moral principles are interpersonally valid. Telling a lie is wrong, no matter who does it. It is wrong for you to tell a lie. It is wrong for John to tell a lie. It is wrong for everyone. If John tells you a lie, it is wrong, even if he thinks there is nothing wrong with lying. You can blame him on the basis of a universalizable moral principle.

This basic point sometimes surprises those who are new to philosophy. They think that ethics is subjective. By "subjective," they usually mean that what is right for me may not be right for you, or that ethics is a matter of personal choice, preference, taste, desire, or opinion. For example, most people agree that non-therapeutic abortion (hereafter, "abortion" for short) is an ethical issue. Some people think that abortion is morally wrong. Others think that abortion is morally permissible (that is, not morally wrong). Those who take ethics to be subjective tend to claim that the moral judgment about abortion depends on personal views. If you are pregnant and wish to terminate the pregnancy, it is your call whether or not abortion is morally permissible. From this, they conclude that the moral judgment about abortion comes down to personal choice.

This train of thought is incorrect. In many countries, women have a legal right to abortion in the first trimester. Legally speaking, they have the right to decide whether they carry the fetus to term or terminate their pregnancy. Within the legal limits, abortion is a matter of personal choice. From this fact, however, it does not follow that the moral judgment about abortion is a matter of personal choice. Deciding what falls under the category of personal choice and what falls under the category of moral judgments is itself an ethical issue. You have to make moral judgments to determine the borderline around personal choice. That is, you must justify the moral judgment that the decision about abortion should be a matter of personal choice. You need a moral argument. You cannot take it for granted that abortion within the first trimester is a matter of personal choice.

Ethics is easily confused with something else. Sometimes ethics is confused with law. But moral judgments are different from legal judgments. For example, some people might think that morally wrong acts are nothing more than those acts that the law prohibits. Killing is illegal, and this is why killing is morally wrong. But insofar as an action is legally permitted, it is morally permissible.

This train of thought is also incorrect. The law does not subsume ethics. Here is an example. Canada is one of the most liberal countries when it comes to non-therapeutic abortion. In most countries where it is legal, abortion beyond the first trimester is not legally permitted unless there is a serious risk to the health of the pregnant woman. In Canada, however, there is no legal restriction on abortion. It is permissible for a woman to request the termination of her pregnancy at any stage. There are only two practical restrictions. First, the termination of the pregnancy must be requested by the woman herself. Second, the abortion must be performed by a registered physician. Furthermore, in most provinces, the public health care system covers the full or partial cost of abortion. Thus, abortion in Canada is legally permissible.

Does this mean that every case of abortion is morally permissible? Clearly, it does not. Suppose a woman requests abortion simply because she prefers a boy to a girl, and a prenatal screening test predicts a baby girl. The reason for this particular request for an abortion is pure prejudice. Is abortion for sexist reasons morally permissible? There are no morally relevant differences between men and women. Abortion on the basis of sexes is a form of discrimination against women. If that is correct, it follows that abortion for purely sexist reasons is morally wrong. Thus, there are some cases of abortion that might be morally wrong. Sometimes legally permitted acts are not morally permissible. It follows that moral judgments are not equivalent to legal judgments.

Sometimes, students ask the following questions: Do the same moral principles apply to all people across different societies? Are there universal moral principles? These questions concern the issue of *relativism*. Simply put, relativism holds that there are no moral principles or judgments that are valid or true in all societies or cultural and historical settings. What is right in one society may not be right in other societies. The debate on relativism goes back a long time in ethics. Some philosophers support relativism. Others reject it and support universal ethics. In this book, we will not take sides. But we do want to point out a difficulty for relativism. If you believe that the truth of moral judgments is relative to particular societies or cultures, you still need to explain what makes them true. For presumably you do not want to say that moral questions can be answered simply by taking a poll. You cannot seriously believe that the view that the majority holds is always automatically right, merely because the people who hold that view outnumber the people who disagree. It is obvious that this cannot be correct.

In any case, relativism does not imply that "anything goes." Relativism is not the view that moral judgments are subjective or arbitrary. Relativists and those who hold that at least some moral principles are universal both believe that moral judgments can be true or false, and that there are good and bad moral arguments.

This point leads us to a more general question: What is distinctive about moral arguments? How can moral claims be defended?

In many respects, moral arguments are similar to other sorts of arguments. They require a valid inference from premises to the conclusion; they are good arguments only if the premises are true and mutually consistent. One thing that is distinct about moral arguments is that they have normative premises: claims about what is good or bad, what ought or ought not to be done. Often, these premises are based on *intuitions* – strong convictions about the rightness (or wrongness) of some kinds of actions that just "seem right" (or wrong).

A lot of ethics is concerned with discovering, clarifying, evaluating, and systematizing intuitions in order to use them in moral arguments. Hence, intuitions need not be arbitrary or unjustified at all. (In this respect, talk of intuitions can be very misleading.) In later chapters, we will engage in the discovery, clarification, evaluation, and systematization of such intuitions. We will engage in moral argument. It is helpful to highlight some of the features and methods that are common in constructing moral arguments.

First, moral argument often uses thought experiments. We have already seen one example of this: the example of the vaccination programs was a thought experiment. It was designed to discover your intuitions in order to identify relevant moral considerations. Thought experiments usually ask you to assume that "other things are equal." This expression is used to simplify an example and enable you to focus on one particular feature. Especially in difficult choices, our students are sometimes tempted to "solve" the question by introducing some additional assumption. We have to tell them that changing the example is against the rules of moral argument.

Here is another example. When we discuss the relevance of age in the allocation of health care resources, we will consider examples where age is the only difference and all other features are equal. An example is:

> Imagine that you are faced with a choice between saving the life of John and saving the life of George. John is 20 years old, and George is 70 years old. Whoever is saved would live for another ten years in full health. Everything else is equal. What is the right thing to do?

As we will discuss in Chapter 4, if your intuition is that John should be saved, then it might reflect the idea that age is a morally relevant consideration in deciding whom to save. If your intuition is that we should be indifferent between (but not towards) saving John's life and George's life, then it might reflect the idea that age is a morally irrelevant consideration. This toy example is set up in such a way that the only difference between the two people is their age. This enables you to focus on the moral relevance or irrelevance of age. This is why you are asked to assume that all the other features are equal. If you assume that George is a Nobel prize winner and John is a criminal, the example becomes more complicated. To avoid complication, you must keep in mind that other things are equal.

Second, we use examples and thought experiments not only to identify intuitions but also to test whether they are consistent. Many people have conflicting intuitions, and the conflict can be discovered by looking at different examples. You have a certain intuition in one example. You consider the idea behind the intuition. Now you are asked to think of another example and to consider what that idea implies in this second example. If you have conflicting intuitions in the two examples, a genuine moral problem arises. You have to find a way to reconcile your intuitions.

Here is a famous illustration. Many people have conflicting intuitions about abortion and infanticide. One is that abortion is morally permissible. The other is that infanticide is morally wrong. Why are these intuitions conflicting? A typical explanation for the permissibility of abortion is that the fetus is not a person. Those who have this view believe that destroying a fetus is different from killing a person. Killing a person is wrong, but destroying a fetus is not wrong. What is the difference between a fetus and a person? One answer is that a fetus does not have self-consciousness whereas a person does. That is, self-consciousness is the criterion for drawing the moral difference between a fetus and a person. But if this idea is correct, how is it possible to justify the intuition that infanticide is morally wrong? A five-day-old newborn does not have self-consciousness. The only difference between a fetus and a newborn is that the fetus is in the womb and the newborn is outside of it. Some infants are born prematurely, sometimes fifteen weeks before the due date; or late, sometimes four weeks after their due date. Thus, the date of birth is an arbitrary cut-off point. Such an arbitrary cut-off point does not suffice to make any moral difference. So there does not seem to be any morally relevant difference between a fetus and a newborn baby. Therefore, the moral judgment about abortion must be the same as the judgment about infanticide: if abortion is morally permissible, then it must be the case that infanticide is also morally permissible.

There are two options now. The first is to give up one of the intuitions. That is, you have to give up either the intuition that abortion is morally permissible or the intuition that infanticide is morally wrong. By giving up either intuition, you can keep the consistency of your moral judgments. The second option is to give up the idea that self-consciousness is the criterion of personhood. If you take this option, you must come up with a different view about what it is to be a person. This is a serious philosophical task. We will not go into it any further. The point is that once you identify your moral intuition in one case, you must ask how far your intuition can go in terms of consistency by testing it in other cases.

You might ask: Why does consistency matter? Why should you want to make your moral beliefs consistent? The answer is that consistency is indispensable in any theory in any academic discipline. Who would believe in an inconsistent theory? A set of inconsistent intuitions is too arbitrary and never constitutes an ethical theory. There is no reason to accept arbitrary moral judgments. This is why one of the main tasks of ethics is to systematize intuitions by justifying them in a coherent moral framework. This is what moral principles and ethical theories attempt to do.

The third feature of moral argument that we need to highlight is the issue of the "burden of proof." Let us stick to the example of abortion and infanticide. Those who think that both abortion and infanticide are morally wrong have consistent judgments on these issues. They argue that infanticide is morally wrong (as many people agree), and that there is no morally relevant difference between a fetus and a newborn baby. It follows, according to their argument, that abortion is morally wrong. There is no inconsistency problem for those who take both abortion and infanticide to be wrong. They do not need to prove anything. The problem is for those who support abortion and reject infanticide. They must establish a morally relevant difference between fetus and newborn if they are not willing to give up one of their intuitions. The burden of proof is on them. Obviously, this does not mean that they have lost the argument.

It just means that the ball is on their side of the court. They have to make the next move.

Let us return to the vaccination example with which we began this chapter. It seems that very few people hold that the only relevant consideration is to maximize the benefits of the vaccination programs, regardless of the way the benefits are distributed. Similarly, few people agree that the only relevant consideration is to give an equal chance of getting the benefits to all the children (which we interpreted as a consideration of fairness). Most of us have the intuition that both benefit maximization and fairness are morally relevant. So the burden of proof is on us to fit these considerations into a coherent moral framework. As a first step, we can try to see how far taking only one of these considerations into account can take us. We will follow this methodology in the next couple of chapters, focusing on benefit maximization. But we will also broaden our analysis as we go along, in part by identifying our intuitions about fairness.

But since the two considerations – benefit maximization and fairness – are commonly thought to fall into different categories of normative concepts, we should briefly introduce these two broad categories. One of them is the category of *deontic* concepts. They include "right" and "wrong," "fair" and "unfair." The other category is that of *axiological* concepts. They include "good" and "bad," "benefit" and "harm."

There are two broadly defined approaches in ethics, corresponding to the way deontic and axiological concepts are related. One approach is *deontology*. According to deontological theories, deontic concepts are independent of axiological concepts. That is, the rightness or wrongness of an act can be determined independently of good and bad – in particular, the goodness or badness of its consequences. The second approach is *consequentialism*. On consequentialist theories, the rightness or wrongness of an act depends solely on the axiological concepts – in particular, the goodness or badness of its consequences. So for consequentialists, right and wrong are solely a matter of consequences; for deontological approaches, right and wrong are a matter of something else. For instance, they may be a matter of individual rights, or they may be a matter of fairness. But it does not follow that the goodness or badness of consequences does not matter for deontology. Most contemporary deontologists accept that the goodness of the consequences of an act is one factor that can affect the ethical status of that act. They just insist that it is not the only factor.

Here is an example. Think of the moral judgment about torture. Many people think that torture is wrong. Why? Typically, there are two types of explanation. The first is that the act of torturing itself is wrong, and that this moral judgment has nothing to do with how much good it would produce. According to this explanation, the act of torturing is wrong under any circumstances, regardless of the goodness of the consequences that torture can bring about. For example, torturing a terrorist who set a bomb to kill innocent people is wrong, even if it is the only way to obtain information on where the bomb is hidden, so that you can defuse the bomb and save the lives of a thousand innocent people. This type of explanation is based on deontology.

The second type of explanation for the wrongness of torture is that the badness of its consequences outweighs the goodness of its consequences. According to this explanation, torture is wrong in most cases, but it is not wrong in some cases when the good effects of torture outweigh its bad effects. For instance, if you can defuse the bomb and save the lives of a thousand innocent people, the goodness of saving the lives of a thousand innocent people can outweigh the badness of the suffering of the terrorist. This type of explanation is based on consequentialism.

The difference between the two approaches can also be thought of in the following way. Consequentialists believe that ethics is about promoting the good. The right act is that which has the best consequences. Deontologists believe that ethics is primarily about complying with duties that may have nothing to do with the goodness of consequences. For them, ethics is concerned with *constraints* on the promotion of the good. Rights and fairness are constraints: an act that would have the best consequences may nevertheless be wrong if it violates a right or if it leads to unfairness.

In this regard, the approach taken in this book is not purely consequentialist. Even though we will argue that the allocation of health care resources should aim at the best consequences – to achieve the best health outcomes – we will also take into account various constraints on the maximization of health benefits. But once again, things are more complicated: perhaps at a higher level of abstraction, deontic concepts, such as fairness, can be given a consequentialist justification. We will not address this issue. Ultimately, we remain neutral between the two approaches.

One argument that will emerge from the rest of this book is that fairness has a central role in the ethics of health care rationing. The maximization of health benefits is certainly important; however, it must be constrained and qualified by the concern for fairness. The notion of fairness crops up in every stage of this book. But philosophers disagree over what fairness demands in different contexts. Therefore, we do not attempt to give an account of fairness. Rather, we will examine it in different contexts of health care rationing, and then attempt to draw some lessons in the Conclusion.

Chapter summary

Health care rationing is the controlled allocation of health care resources. It is ubiquitous in every health care system, even if rationing choices are not always readily apparent. Because of the scarcity of health care resources, rationing is also inevitable. Health care rationing is an ethical issue, and it needs to be governed by ethical principles. Two relevant, basic moral ideas are the maximization of the benefits from the use of health care resources and the fairness of the distribution of those benefits.

Discussion questions

1. "The health care system and health insurance markets are regulated by the government. In many countries, democratically elected politicians run the government. The decision concerning health care rationing should therefore be made by politicians. We do not need any ethical principle for rationing health care." Do you agree with this argument? Why or why not?

2. Imagine that you are in a position of making decisions about the use of health care resources. You have $100,000 in hand. You can use it either to fund an expensive treatment of a rare form of disease for Jessica – a young child whose plight has been presented on national television – or you can use the money to fund a public health program to reduce children's risk of the exposure to lead paint. Statistically, the program is expected to save the lives of two children, who are not yet identified. Some people value helping an identifiable victim more than a statistical victim, hence preferring to use the funds to help Jessica. Is such a bias toward identifiable victims ethically justifiable?

3. As we mentioned in Section 1.3, the overuse of antibiotics might lead to the emergence of resistant strains of bacteria. Suppose you are asked by the World Health Organization to come up with strategies to reduce the overuse of antibiotics. What policies would you recommend?

4. Many people are upset by the idea of rationing health care. At the same time, funding bodies regularly set priorities in the allocation of funds for medical research. This is a form of rationing too. Medical research can benefit patients, but when some research projects get low priority, some patients can be disadvantaged. Yet no one objects to the controlled allocation of resources for medical research. Is rationing more acceptable in the setting of research priorities than in health care? Why or why not? What is the moral difference between them?

5. People disagree about many moral questions, and there is a great diversity of moral beliefs among different cultures. Do you think that the facts of disagreements and diversity provide an argument for moral relativism? Why or why not?

6. When Seattle's Swedish Hospital started offering kidney dialysis to a limited number of outpatients in 1962, a committee consisting of laypeople was set up to make decisions concerning who should receive

the treatment among a pool of needy patients. This committee became known as the *God Committee*. The following is a part of the committee members' discussion, famously reported in Alexander (1962: 110). What are reasonable, or unreasonable, points in this discussion?

LAWYER: The doctors have told us they will soon have two more vacancies at the Kidney Center, and they have submitted a list of five candidates for us to choose from.

HOUSEWIFE: Are they all equally sick?

Dr. MURRAY (John A. Murray, M.D., Medical Director of the Kidney Center): Patients Number One and Number Five can last only a couple more weeks. The others probably can go a bit longer. But for purposes of your selection, all five cases should be considered of equal urgency, because none of them can hold out until another treatment facility becomes available.

LAWYER: Are there any preliminary ideas?

BANKER: Just to get the ball rolling, why don't we start with Number One – the housewife from Walla Walla.

SURGEON: This patient could not commute for the treatment from Walla Walla, so she would have to find a way to move her family to Seattle.

BANKER: Exactly my point. It says here that her husband has no funds to make such a move.

LAWYER: Then you are proposing we eliminate this candidate on the grounds that she could not possibly accept treatment if it were offered?

MINISTER: How can we compare a family situation of two children, such as this woman in Walla Walla, with a family of six children such as patient Number Four – the aircraft worker?

STATE OFFICIAL: But are we sure the aircraft worker can be rehabilitated? I note he is already too ill to work, whereas Number Two and Number Five, the chemist and the accountant, are both still able to keep going.

LABOR LEADER: I know from experience that the aircraft company where this man works will do everything possible to rehabilitate a handicapped employee ...

HOUSEWIFE: If we are still looking for the men with the highest potential of service to society, I think we must consider that the chemist and the accountant have the finest educational backgrounds of all five candidates.

SURGEON: How do the rest of you feel about Number Three – the small businessman with three children? I am impressed that his doctor took special pains to mention this man is active in church work. This is an indication to me of character and moral strength.

HOUSEWIFE: Which certainly would help him conform to the demands of the treatment ...

LAWYER: It would also help him to endure a lingering death ...

STATE OFFICIAL: But that would seem to be placing a penalty on the very people who perhaps have the most provident ...

MINISTER: And both these families have three children too.

LABOR LEADER: For the children's sake, we've got to reckon with the surviving parents' opportunity to remarry, and a woman with three children has a better chance to find a new husband than a very young widow with six children.

SURGEON: How can we possibly be sure of that? ...

Further readings

The vaccination program example is discussed in the context of HIV/ AIDS and in much more detail by Johansson and Norheim (2011). The example originally comes from Daniel Wikler, who generously agreed to lend it to us. The problem of abortion and infanticide is introduced by Tooley (1972). If you have never studied ethics before, a good introduction is Driver (2007). Timmons (2013) is a slightly more advanced, but also more detailed, introduction.

2   The value of health

2.1 Well-being and health

The rationing of health care resources includes the controlled allocation of things such as subsidies for medicines, operating costs for hospitals, places on waiting lists, organs for transplantation, or funds for public health programs and medical research. It also involves deciding which interventions and services should be covered by health insurance packages. In emergencies, it might be necessary to ration beds in intensive care units, vaccines in areas affected by epidemics, or emergency medical personnel to different locations. These allocation choices must be efficient and fair: they must lead to the best consequences while taking into account relevant moral constraints. But the things that are allocated are very different. How can we decide which ones of the many possible allocations are fair and do the most good?

The answer to this question may at first seem straightforward. The objective of health care is to restore and maintain health and to prevent and alleviate suffering due to ill-health. Obviously, you cannot literally redistribute health itself. Unlike income, health cannot be taken from one person and given to another. You cannot restore a patient's health by taking some health from someone else and giving it to her. Still, you might be able to use health as a *metric* to compare different resource allocations. You can try to measure the degree to which different allocations contribute to restoring and maintaining health. Thus, you might be able to say that heart surgeries do more to restore and maintain health than hip replacements. They are more important, so they should have higher priority.

But this answer faces a difficulty. Health is not some sort of natural quantity that can be measured on a common scale – as opposed to distance or blood pressure. Compare a person who has poor eyesight to another who has poor hearing. Neither of them can function as well as others. Both of them fall short of what is typical of healthy human beings. But which of them falls short *more*? Which of them is more unhealthy? Good health is made up of many kinds of physical, biological, mental, and psychological functions, which do not have a common metric. You cannot simply look at the "amount" of health that people have, because health does not come in one sort of quantity. To be sure, some comparisons are easy enough to make: a person who has asthma or a broken arm is less healthy than a person in perfect health. But other comparisons seem intractably difficult. Are you less healthy if you have asthma or if you have migraines? If you have a broken arm or a broken leg? If you are deaf or if you are blind?

Consequently, you cannot compare alternative uses of health care resources by measuring the extent to which they contribute to restoring and maintaining health or to preventing ill-health. It is impossible to directly compare different aspects of health. There is no metric of health that helps you determine whether asthma medication restores functioning to a greater degree than back pain medication. They restore different functions. If you have to choose between providing asthma medication or back pain medication, you cannot make your choice by determining which makes people more healthy. Both asthma and back pain medication can improve health, but it is not possible to directly determine which leads to a greater improvement.

Some readers may find this argument too hasty. After all, surely asthma is worse than back pain. Breaking a leg leaves you worse off than breaking an arm. Being deaf is less of a disadvantage than being blind.

These comparisons may or may not be true. But the thing to note is that they are not comparisons of health. They are not claims about which conditions represent more or less health. Rather, they are comparisons of *value*. What they say is that it is *worse* to be with some of these conditions than with others. So they provide no objection to our argument. Instead, when people make such claims, what they mean is that a condition is worse when it makes life more difficult, when it leads to less well-being, when it creates disadvantage. The distinction is important. It is one thing to try to measure health; it is another to measure the *value* of health.

Fortunately, a measure of health is not needed for the purposes of resource allocation. For, ultimately, we do not much care about health itself. What we do care about is its value for us: the way it affects our well-being or quality of life. (In this book, we use these terms interchangeably.) Disease and injury lead to a loss of quality of life: they cause pain, they worsen functioning, they shorten lives. The point of medical interventions and health care services is to make life better by alleviating pain, restoring functioning and extending it. Consequently, when we allocate health care resources, we should be interested in their impact on quality of life. In other words, what matters is the impact of health on well-being.

Of course, the next question is what well-being is. Unfortunately, there is no generally accepted theory in philosophy. There are many rival theories. Fortunately, however, we can remain neutral between them. Here's why. No one would deny that health makes a major contribution to our well-being. As philosophers say, it has *instrumental value* for us. On any plausible theory, health will be important because of its instrumental value. But on some theories, health will additionally have *intrinsic value*: good health in itself is one of those things that make life good. On these views, health is part of well-being. Whichever kind of view you take, health will be important. So, we can remain noncommittal in this book about theories of well-being, since our interest is in health. More precisely, our interest is in *health-related quality of life*: that fraction of overall well-being that is determined by health. To discuss it, we do not have to take a view on whether health has intrinsic or instrumental value. For simplicity, we shall simply say that health is a *component* of well-being, leaving it open whether it just contributes to it or is itself part of it.

Let us take stock. We have argued for the following so far. The allocation of health care resources is an ethical problem. Because scarcity is inevitable, resources should be distributed in a way that does the most good. (Another aim, to be addressed as we go along, is that they be distributed fairly.) As it is often put, the utilization of health care resources should provide "the best value for money." But how do you find out which interventions and services provide better value for money than others? A straightforward answer is that you can do this by measuring health. But health is not a quantity; it involves many functions which are impossible to compare. So you have to proceed indirectly, by measuring the value of health – its impact on quality of life. Other things being equal, an intervention provides more value if it has a greater positive impact on quality of life. The more it increases health-related quality of life, the greater its value.

We should note that not everyone agrees with the way we think of well-being and health. For example, the World Health Organization (WHO) defines health as "a state of complete physical, mental, and social well-being, and not merely the absence of disease or infirmity."[1] Our view about well-being and health is incompatible with this definition of health. But we should not accept this definition. For one thing, it is implausibly expansive: it *identifies* health with well-being. But, obviously, there are other things beside health that contribute to physical, mental, and social well-being. Happiness and an adequate material standard of living are two plausible candidates. The WHO's definition would turn them into matters of health. We should be more modest: health is valuable because it is a component of well-being, not because it exhausts it. When we measure the value of health, we do not measure all of well-being.

Yet there is a serious difficulty for our view that the ethics of health care rationing should focus on health-related quality of life. The view assumes that you can put a value on the impact of health on overall well-being – that you can measure health-related quality of life independently of other components of well-being. But this requires that you can separate the contribution of health to well-being from the contribution of other components. It requires that you can take a measure of a person's overall well-being and tell how much of it is due to her happiness, standard of living, health, and so on.

We are sure it can immediately be seen that it is very unlikely that well-being can be measured this way. Even if you could independently measure health-related quality of life, happiness-related quality of life, standard of living, and so on, it is incredible that well-being is simply the sum of them, or that they can be put together in some other simple way to make up overall well-being. This is because different components of well-being interact: their impacts are inseparable from one another. Asthma is worse for someone who enjoys working outdoors. A finger injury is worse for a concert pianist than an opera singer. Back pain is worse for someone who takes care of small children than someone who works in an office. The value of health is not separable from the value of other components of well-being.

This problem is widely recognized. No one disputes that the impact of health cannot be separated from the impact of other components of well-being. But there is much less agreement on how serious the problem is. Some philosophers have argued that since we cannot evaluate health as a component of well-being, we should simply give up and try to measure overall well-being instead. We could then choose between alternative resource allocations by determining which makes the lives of people go best, all things considered.

But it seems a bit extravagant to try to allocate health care resources by taking into account all the different ways in which health can interact with other components of well-being. Consider just the information needs of such a proposal. The effectiveness of every intervention and medical procedure would depend not only on how they improve functioning, whether they remove all symptoms, or how many years they add to a patient's life, but also on how important the improvement of a particular function is for the particular patient, how it would affect that patient's happiness, standard of living, or any other component of her well-being. You would have to collect all this information for every single patient! Needless to say, this would be prohibitively costly.

This is not to say that such information is never relevant. A physician in a hospital or in general practice can and should take into account the impact of a condition and its treatment on particular patients, with their different values and circumstances. But in the allocation of health care resources, our focus is on populations. We need to abstract away from the differences of individual patients, and consider the badness of a condition in general terms. We should acknowledge that any measure of health-related quality of life is an approximation. While the inseparability problem cannot be avoided, a measure of health-related quality of life can be interpreted as expressing the typical or average impact of health on well-being. After all, it sounds plausible that on first approximation a broken wrist is just as bad for you as for me. Of course, on second look, it may be worse for you if you are a concert pianist. But even though every patient is different, in large-scale resource allocation choices we are forced to abstract away from such individual differences.

2.2 Health-related quality of life

How can we put a value on the impact of health on well-being? How can we measure health-related quality of life? Consider particular diseases and injuries. Diabetes, asthma, depression, or HIV have very different impacts on a patient's life. They affect differently the way a patient is able to function biologically, psychologically, or socially. How can we express their impact in a single, summary value?

Broadly speaking, there are two approaches. In this section and the next, we present the most commonly used approach. In Section 2.4, we present an alternative.

The first approach focuses on *health states* rather than particular diseases and injuries. A health state is a description of different levels of functioning that patients can achieve in the presence of particular health conditions. It is a constellation of different functional limitations. Rather than measuring the badness of particular conditions, this approach evaluates health states directly. To see how this works, consider the EQ-5D, a widely used questionnaire for describing health states. It is reproduced here as Figure 2.1.

As apparent at first glance, this is a very simple questionnaire. Patients are asked to describe how well they function within five "dimensions" or aspects of health. Their answers to the questions define their health state. For instance, a patient who has no problems with walking, self-care, and performing daily activities, but has moderate pain and anxiety, will be in a different health state than a patient who has some problems walking, washing and dressing, and performing other daily activities, but no pain or anxiety.

The EQ-5D is intended to be simple, easy to fill out, and quick. It includes only five dimensions of health. It does not allow fine discrimination between different levels of functioning within these dimensions — in this version, there are only three descriptions to choose from. Even so, notice the large number of health states that can be described:

three levels in five dimensions defines $3^5 = 243$ different health states! The five-level version of the EQ-5D, which allows two additional levels of functioning for the five dimensions, describes 3,125 different health states. Even more detailed instruments are able to differentiate between tens of thousands of health states.

There are countless similar questionnaires. Some of them are general; others are targeted to the circumstances of particular patient groups. Some focus on the health outcomes of particular treatments and interventions. Some of them are short and simple, like the EQ-5D; others are longer and much more comprehensive.

It is important to note that the health states defined by the EQ-5D and similar questionnaires are simply descriptions. When a patient ticks the first box for the first three questions, and the second for the last two, her health state is very different from the health state of a patient who ticks the second box for the first three questions, and the first box for the last two. But based on this information, you cannot tell whose health-related quality of life is lower. The health states still need to be evaluated.

By placing a tick in one box in each group below, please indicate which statements best describe your own health state today.
- Mobility
  - ☐ I have no problems in walking about
  - ☐ I have some problems in walking about
  - ☐ I am confined to bed
- Self-Care
  - ☐ I have no problems with self-care
  - ☐ I have some problems washing or dressing myself
  - ☐ I am unable to wash or dress myself
- Usual Activities (e.g. work, study, housework, family or leisure activities)
  - ☐ I have no problems with performing my usual activities
  - ☐ I have some problems with performing my usual activities
  - ☐ I am unable to perform my usual activities
- Pain/Discomfort
  - ☐ I have no pain or discomfort
  - ☐ I have moderate pain or discomfort
  - ☐ I have extreme pain or discomfort
- Anxiety/Depression
  - ☐ I am not anxious or depressed
  - ☐ I am moderately anxious or depressed
  - ☐ I am extremely anxious or depressed

Figure 2.1 The EQ-5D (3L) questionnaire.

Thus, the respondents are given a second task. They are presented with a vertical scale that looks very much like a thermometer. It has a hundred grades, numbered in increments of 5 between 0 and 100, where 100 is defined as "the best health you can imagine," and 0 is defined as "the worst health you can imagine." The respondents are asked to put a mark on the scale that indicates their current health. Thus, in the first step, the researchers learn the health state a respondent is currently in. In the second step, they learn how she evaluates that health state.

Suppose there are three respondents. The first one has no problem in any of the dimensions in the questionnaire. She rates her health as 100. The second respondent has some problems with performing daily activities and some moderate pain or discomfort, but she has no problems with mobility and self-care, and she is not anxious or depressed. This respondent rates her own health at 76. The third respondent ticked the middle box for all the questions: she has some problems with walking, self-care, and other daily activities, and she is also in moderate pain and moderately depressed. She gives the value of 52 to her own health.

We now have evaluations of three health states. For the sake of simplicity, we can put these values on a scale between 0 and 1, where full health has the value of 1 and the worst imaginable health state, not better than death, has the value of 0. Thus, the health-related quality of life of the first respondent is 1; the health-related quality of life of the second respondent is 0.76; and the health-related quality of life of the third respondent is 0.52. (Of course, in practice, values like 0.52 and 0.76 are averages, since they are determined by the responses of many people. Thus, researchers do not have to repeat the second task each time. The transformations from descriptions to valuations are already available from previous studies.)

The method for establishing quality of life values for health states that we have just presented is called the *rating scale* method. It is simple to administer for researchers and easy to understand for respondents. But it has a serious limitation.

In our example, 0.76 is associated with the health state characterized by some problems with performing daily activities, some moderate pain, but no problems in any of the other dimensions; 0.52 is associated with the health state characterized by some problems with walking, self-care, daily activities, and moderate pain and depression. Based on these values, the first health state is less bad than the second. Patients in this health state have a higher health-related quality of life than patients in the second. But can we say anything more than this?

Imagine that these states are the health outcomes for particular patients with and without treatment. Patient A is currently in the first health state: her health-related quality of life is 0.76. You can, however, provide a treatment to her that would restore her to full health – to the health-related quality of life of 1. The treatment would alleviate her pain and restore her ability to carry out daily activities. Patient B's health-related quality of life is currently 0.52. You can also treat her, but you cannot restore her to full health. All you can do for her is restore her mobility and ability to care for herself, as well as curing her depression. But she will be left with some moderate pain and problems with carrying out usual daily activities. The health outcome of her treatment would be the first health state with health-related quality of life at 0.76. Now the question is: Which treatment would result in a greater improvement?

A simple answer is that the improvements are the same. Patient A would improve from 0.76 to 1. Patient B would improve from 0.52 to 0.76. The increases look the same – 0.24 in both cases.

But the simple answer is wrong. On the basis of the rating scale method, you *cannot* claim that the increases represent the same improvement in health-related quality of life. You cannot say this because the method establishes a ranking only. The *differences* between the values of this ranking do not have any meaning. They cannot be interpreted as measures of improvement.

The rating scale method provides very little information – it provides only a ranking of health states. To decide whether A and B would achieve the same degree of health-related quality of life improvement, a more precise scale is needed. You need a scale on which the *intervals* between different values can be compared.

To be fair, some researchers argue that the rating scale method does provide you with a scale on which such comparisons are possible. But this is extremely controversial. It is mysterious how having people indicating values on a thermometer-like scale could take you from a ranking to a measure with which the differences between values can be compared. The respondents only provide their rankings. How can you be certain that those rankings carry the necessary information for interval comparisons?

Plainly, you need a test for this. Researchers have developed methods to elicit the sort of valuation from respondents that make the construction of more precise scales possible. These can be used to test the values elicited by the rating scale method. But at this point, the whole problem seems to go away. For notice that once you use the other methods to test the rating scale method, you can simply go ahead and use these methods for the evaluation of health states directly. There is no need for rating scales.

What makes it possible to construct more precise measures on the other elicitation methods is that they use comparisons from the start. Respondents do not directly evaluate health states. Instead, they are asked to make trade-offs between living with different health outcomes. Their evaluation of any particular health state is indirect.

One of the best-known methods is called the *standard gamble*. In this method, respondents are given a health state description. For example, they are told that in one health state, patients have some moderate pain and discomfort, as well as some problems with performing usual daily activities. Then they are asked to make a choice. On the one hand, they can choose to live in this health state for a certain amount of time. (For example, ten years followed by instant death.) On the other hand, they can choose to receive a treatment that will either restore them to full health with some probability p for the same amount of time, or lead to instant death with probability $(1 - p)$. Respondents have to determine the value for p at which they are indifferent between the two options. At this point, they would be just about as willing to take the gamble as to live in the health state.

In other words, p is varied until the respondents are indifferent. Suppose at this point p is 0.76. Respondents would be willing to risk death in order to be cured, as long as they have at least as great of a chance of survival as this. To put it a bit imprecisely, their responses reveal the *relative* value they place on the health state compared to full health and death. (More precisely, it reveals the relative value they place on the *differences* between the health state and full health, and the health state and death.)

We have now established the value of the health state characterized by some moderate pain and some problems with performing usual daily activities. It is 0.76. We can substitute any health state description in the question to determine its value. For instance, suppose that respondents are indifferent between living in a health state characterized by some problems with walking, self-care, and daily activities as well as moderate pain and depression, and a "treatment gamble" in which they have a 52 percent chance of being restored to full health and a 48 percent chance of instant death. The value of this health state is 0.52.

The health-related quality of life level for these two health states are 0.76 and 0.52. Evidently, the second health state is worse than the first – people would be willing to take a greater risk to avoid it. But unlike before, these values provide us with a more precise scale for measuring health-related quality of life. Since they are based on trade-offs, these are relative values. They allow for comparisons of *changes* in health-related quality of life.

Return to our patients A and B. A's health-related quality of life is 0.76; B's is 0.52. You can return A to full health or you can improve B's condition from 0.52 to 0.76. The question was which treatment results in a greater health-related quality of life improvement. Armed with the scale provided by the standard gamble method, you can now say that the change from 0.52 to 0.76 and the change from 0.76 to 1 represent equal improvements – that is, they represent changes of the same magnitude in health-related quality of life. To put it a bit more technically, the

standard gamble yields an interval scale that carries much more information than mere rankings. In particular, the ratio of differences – intervals
on the scale – can be compared.

If the standard gamble looks a bit complicated, that's because it is. It
can be time consuming to explain and administer, and its critics complain that it is not easy for research participants to understand. A similar
but simpler method is the *time trade-off* method.

This time, the respondent is not faced with risky choices. Rather, she
has to determine how much time (typically, in years of life) she would be
willing to give up to avoid living in a health state that is worse than full
health. Let us take our stock example again: on the one hand, a person
can live for T years with some problems with performing daily activities
and some moderate pain; on the other hand, she can live for X years in
full health. Plainly, $X < T$, since it is better to spend a given amount of
time in full health than to spend the same amount of time with less than
full health. Consequently, the value of the health state is determined by
X/T. For instance, if respondents consider 7.6 years in full health just as
good as 10 years with some problems with performing daily activities and
some moderate pain, then the value of this health state is 0.76.

The time trade-off method yields the same sort of scale as the standard
gamble. It also allows comparing the magnitudes of different improvements
in health-related quality of life. Because it does not involve probabilities, it
might be a bit easier to understand for respondents. But it is still more
complicated than the rating scale method. Nonetheless, the standard
gamble and the time trade-off have an advantage. When you are seriously
ill, you might have to make trade-offs between longevity and health, or take
"gambles" between risky treatments. In other words, many patients in real
life are faced with just these sorts of choices. From this perspective, the
standard gamble and the time trade-off look more realistic than directly
estimating the value of health states on some thermometer-like visual scale.

Earlier, we said that the rating scale method is unlikely to provide an
interval scale. But if it yields fairly similar valuations, then perhaps you
could argue that it can be used as a convenient shortcut to avoid the more
complicated elicitation methods. As it happens, this is a much more
controversial and complicated issue than it seems, with notoriously per-
sistent disagreements between different researchers. Here are some results
from one study that focused on functional limitations on the ability to
walk unaided. One of the health states that was examined was described
as "needing a walking stick when walking." Using the standard gamble,
health-related quality of life in this health state is 0.85; using the time
trade-off method, it is 0.78; and using the rating scale method, it is 0.65.
In general, it seems that the values are lowest on the rating scale, and
considerably higher on the time trade-off method and the standard

gamble, with the latter yielding the highest values. Just what to conclude from these results is not entirely clear. But perhaps they suggest that the rating scale method is indeed problematic: when they are not forced to consider the need to make sacrifices and trade-offs, people tend to over-estimate the badness of health states.

Nevertheless, both the standard gamble and the time trade-off method face their own problem. Admittedly, these problems are a bit technical. We will not go into them in detail. But the basic ideas are not difficult to understand.

Consider the time trade-off method first. In this method, respondents have to determine how many years of life they would be willing to give up to avoid living in a health state that is worse than full health. In the example we have worked with, respondents consider 7.6 years in full health just as good as 10 years in a health state marked by some problems with performing daily activities and some moderate pain. Therefore, the value of this health state is 0.76.

But this conclusion relies on a crucial assumption. The method assumes that when people consider their future health, their evaluations are not distorted by how far they look ahead in the future. To use the technical term, they do not *discount* their future health.

If people discount their future health, then they value good health in the near future more than good health in the further future. They put a greater value on avoiding a bad health state next year than ten years from now. (Whether this is rational is a separate question that we will not take up here.) The problem is that if people do discount future health, then when they consider 7.6 years in full health just as good as ten years in a worse health state, their valuation may be distorted, because they put a smaller value on health in the further future. They would, for example, place the value of 0.5 only on the health state in itself. But since it appears less bad to them in the further future, the time trade-off that they are willing to make *now* makes the health state look less bad. So you get a distorted result.

This would not be a problem if you knew whether your respondents discount future health. If you knew the rate at which they discount, you could take it into account. But in practice, time trade-off studies have to assume that people do not discount future health at all. Perhaps the assumption is correct. But you cannot find this out from time trade-off questions. Hence you need the assumption.

The problem facing the standard gamble is similar. In this method, people make risky choices between treatment options. The outcomes of these choices are different health states. The method assumes that when respondents consider the options, their choices are determined only by the severity of those health states, rather than the risk itself. More technically, it is assumed that people's risk-attitudes towards different health states are constant. For instance, they do not become more sensitive to risk when they consider worse health states. The results will be distorted if respondents have different levels of willingness to take risks. Just as someone who has $10 and someone who has $1,000 might differ in their willingness to take gambles with their money, people's willingness to take risks with their health might depend on their own health state.

Again, you will not be able to find out from the responses to standard gamble questions whether respondents have the same risk-attitude in different choices. That is why you need to make an assumption.

What should we conclude from the discussion of these problems? On the one hand, it would be easy to become pessimistic about the prospects of measuring the value of health. The rating scale method suffers from a credibility problem: it is hard to believe that people can evaluate the badness of different health states at the required level of precision merely by placing them on a thermometer-like scale. The standard gamble has to assume that people have a constant risk-attitude towards health. The time trade-off method has to assume that people do not discount future health. These assumptions can be questioned.

On the other hand, we should realize that we cannot do without measuring health-related quality of life. It would be impossible to allocate health care resources efficiently and fairly without it. It is true that none of the methods for measuring the value of health are free of problems. Each of them requires simplifying assumptions. But health state valuations are approximations. It is inevitable that some imprecision will creep into them.

One thing to ask is how severe these imprecisions are. There are two sorts of answer to this question. First, we can test our methods. Researchers have looked at the consistency between the results given by the same respondents for repeated questions, as well as the consistency of the results from different groups of respondents. Overall, they have found that the responses are fairly consistent – as statisticians put it, they are reliable. This is good news, since it gives us some confidence that our measurements are close to the truth.

The second answer is to remind ourselves that we should not expect a perfect measure. Social science is seldom as exact as the natural sciences. Measuring health-related quality of life is especially difficult, but its difficulties are still less severe than the difficulties faced by other measures of well-being. Consider, for instance, measuring the gross domestic product (GDP) of a country. Think of the simplifications, approximations, and assumptions that go into calculating a country's GDP! The assumptions that must be made when measuring health-related quality of life seem mild indeed compared to them. Yet GDP is regularly used to represent a country's "economic health," and policies are regularly evaluated by their expected impact on GDP.

For another example, consider the Human Development Index, a measure of the well-being of the population in a country used by the United Nations Development Programme and other organizations. It takes into account life expectancy at birth, mean years of schooling and expected years of schooling, and gross national income per capita. It was designed to overcome the limitations of GDP as a measure of well-being. Yet it is obviously a very crude measure. But that does not mean it is useless. Rather, you should keep in mind its limitations when you use it. The same applies to measures of health-related quality of life. They must play a role in health care resource allocation. But their limitations must be kept in mind.

2.3 Quality-adjusted measures

Suppose you are interested in the health of populations. Perhaps you want to compare the health of people living in two different countries. Or you want to compare the health of people in two socioeconomic groups within one country. You notice that one bad thing that disease and injury do to people is shortening their lives by killing them. Since longevity is valuable, you might decide to make these comparisons by looking at how long the people in these groups live.

But it is unclear what "how long people live" means. A population is made up of people of different ages. So you have to look at some average. But even that is insufficient. People in your population are still alive, so you have to look at how long they can *expect* to live.

It is customary to take life expectancy as a simple measure of health. But since people in your population are at different ages, they obviously have different life expectancies, even on average. Ten-year-old children have a different average life expectancy than 50-year-old adults. So what you could focus on is *life expectancy at birth*.

This is a familiar and widely used measure (it is one component of the Human Development Index, mentioned above). Suppose you discover that the population of one country has a higher average life expectancy at birth than the population of another country. You might also believe it is unfair that there are such differences in people's life prospects. You might argue that it is a matter of justice to help the second country to increase average life expectancy. Similarly, you might discover that people in a more advantaged socioeconomic group within one country can expect to live longer than people belonging to a less advantaged socioeconomic group. You might then argue it is a matter of justice to help the more disadvantaged have better life prospects.

Your argument is based, in both cases, on some moral principle and a simple measure of well-being – in this case, a measure of health-related quality of life, one component of well-being. You could not apply your moral principle if you did not have some measure like that. In fact, in the absence of a measure, you would not even be able to identify the states of affairs that you can consider unfair. You *must* use a measure, despite the methodological difficulties discussed in the previous sections.

But life expectancy at birth is a very crude approximation of well-being, or even only of health-related quality of life. It provides too little information. It tells you about the "quantity" of life that people can expect to have, but it does not tell you anything about its quality. It does not tell you how healthy people are during their life. A better measure would take into account the quality of life as well as its quantity.

Fortunately, the health state evaluations that we have been discussing can be used for just this purpose. In the previous section, we looked at how you can assign values to different health states on a scale between 0 and 1. We interpreted 1 as full health. Now we can extend that interpretation: let 1 stand for *spending one year in full health*. Let values that are smaller than 1 stand for *spending one year in a health state that is worse than full health*. (Taking one year as the unit is yet another simplification.) This way, when you look at the health states that people can expect to be in throughout their years of life, you can assign values to them. Any year spent in full health has the value of 1; any year spent in less than full health has a value that is *adjusted* by the health-related quality of life for the health state during that year.

This is the measure of *health-adjusted life expectancy* (HALE). Suppose a person, at birth, can expect to live for 75 years. For most of her life, she can be expected to be completely healthy. In the last ten years, however, she can expect to suffer from chronic conditions. For five years, she can expect to have some problems with performing daily activities and to live with some moderate pain. Her health-related quality of life will be only 0.76 during this period. And for the last five years of her life she can also expect to have some problems with walking and self-care, as well as being moderately depressed. Her health-related quality of life in these five years will be 0.52.

Her health-adjusted life expectancy is easy to calculate. She expects to spend 65 years in full health. Each of these years has a value of 1. Then she can expect to spend five years at the health-related quality of life level 0.76, followed by five years at 0.52. So her HALE is

$$65 \times 1 + 5 \times 0.76 + 5 \times 0.52 = 71.4.$$

Therefore, even though this person's life expectancy at birth is 75 years, her health-adjusted life expectancy at birth is only 71.4 years.

Obviously, there are going to be differences between people in any population. But at least in principle, the data for health-adjusted life expectancies can be collected. They can provide a more precise way to compare the populations of different countries and socioeconomic groups.

Moreover, the idea behind health-adjusted life expectancy can be further extended. It can be applied to any health outcome, including outcomes associated with particular interventions and treatments for different conditions. This general measure is called *quality-adjusted life year* (QALY).

A QALY is a combination of health-related quality of life and years of life: 1 QALY can represent one year of life in full health; or it can represent two years at health-related quality of life level 0.5; or it can represent four years at 0.25. For example, suppose that one treatment for cancer patients provides five years of remission at the health-related quality of life level of 0.4, while another treatment provides three years of remission at 0.7. The outcome of the first treatment is 2 QALYs; the outcome of the second treatment is 2.1 QALYs. The second treatment, taking into account both health-related quality of life and quantity of life, is more valuable. It results in more QALYs.

Note that quality-adjusted measures assume that the value of a health state is proportional to its duration. This does not seem an unreasonable assumption to us. But perhaps it does not always hold. For the time being, we can treat it as another simplifying assumption. If it turns out to be unrealistic, it can be modified.

QALYs enable us to compare all sorts of resource uses in health care. They can represent the value of the health outcomes of different treatments and interventions. They can represent the value of public health programs. They can be used to evaluate the health of particular patients, or patient groups, or even whole populations. In the next chapter, we will take a more detailed look at how they can help us make choices in health care priority setting.

2.4 The burden of disease

At the beginning of Section 2.2, we said there were two approaches to health-related quality of life measurement. The first focuses on the impact of ill-health on the different ways a person functions, defining health states in terms of shortfalls in functioning. This approach forms the foundation of QALYs.

The other approach focuses on diseases, injuries, and risk factors. It begins from a distinction introduced by the World Health Organization – the distinction between impairment, disability, and handicap. An *impairment* is the loss or abnormality in physiological, psychological, or anatomical functioning that is the direct consequence of disease or injury.

It can be described in biomedical terms. A *disability* is a loss or restriction of ability, as a result of the impairment, to carry out an activity that is considered normal for human beings. And a *handicap* is the disadvantage that results from the impairment or disability that limits or prevents the individual to fulfill her role in her economic, social, and cultural environment. (The WHO no longer uses this distinction. Nevertheless, we think it remains useful for introducing the ideas below.)

When we evaluate the badness of different conditions, we can consider them as impairments, disabilities, or handicaps. But if we evaluate them merely as impairments, we are unlikely to capture their impact on well-being. And if we evaluate them as handicaps, there is going to be too much variation depending on the economic, social, and cultural circumstances of different people and populations. In order to find a middle ground between taking into account too little and too much information, we should evaluate them as disabilities.

This is the approach taken by the Global Burden of Disease project – an international attempt to measure the harm from mortality and morbidity from disease and injury in the populations of different countries and regions of the world. The harms, or the "burdens", of hundreds of conditions are measured on a common scale and they are aggregated into a summary value for a given population. The conditions range from mild hearing loss, through alcohol use disorder and HIV/AIDS, to acute schizophrenia.

The measure developed by the Global Burden of Disease project is called *disability-adjusted life year* (DALY). The basic idea is similar to the QALY, but the details are different. Since the primary interest of the developers of the DALY was in the harm associated with different conditions – rather than the benefit associated with different interventions – DALYs represent the gap between actual health and some ideal level of health. The gap can be caused both by losing years of life because of disease or injury, and by having to live with a disability. DALYs are a combination of *years of life lost* due to disability and *years of life lived with a disability*.

Let us explain. One of the harms of diseases and injuries is premature death – shortening people's lives. If a person is killed by a disease at age 50, one way to represent the harm is to take the difference between the number of years that she has lived and the number of years that she could have lived. But for this, you obviously need to be able to estimate how many more years this person could have lived. One way to do this would be to take the average life expectancy at 50 in the population to which this person belonged. But this leads to a problem: do you really want to say that the death of a 50-year-old person who belongs to a population where average life expectancy is 60 is *less bad* than the death of a person at the same age who belongs to a population where average life expectancy is 80?

The developers of the DALY offered another solution. They argued that the harm of premature mortality should be estimated not on the basis of how many more years a person could have lived in the particular population to which she belonged, but on the basis of what human beings could achieve under reasonably ideal conditions. This way, the harm of dying at 50 is the same no matter where a person lives, since it depends on how long people could ideally live. Of course, you cannot say for certain how many years that would be, but you can look at the population with the greatest life expectancy in the world. You can treat the life expectancy in the population that achieves the greatest life expectancy at birth as the ideal life expectancy for all human beings. Under present conditions, living less than that is the harm caused by premature mortality.

The country with the greatest life expectancy is Japan. In the early 1990s, at the time the Global Burden of Disease studies began, life expectancy at birth in Japan was 82.5 years for females and 80 years for males. Thus, the ideal age to which premature death was compared was set to 82.5 years for females and 80 years for males. The difference between men and women was attributed to the different survival potential of the sexes, which is thought to be at least in part biologically determined. Thus, if a person dies at 50, the burden of premature mortality was the same regardless of whether this person lived in one of the most advanced nations or one of the least developed countries. The only factor that made a difference was the person's sex.

You might want to stop us at this point. You might wonder why there should be different ideal life expectancies for men and women. You might argue that even if men are naturally disposed to have shorter lives – or, perhaps just as importantly, they are more willing to take risks with their own health – this should not make a difference to the burden of premature death. It should not be less bad if a man dies at 50 than if a woman does.

You would be right to make this argument. Mostly for this reason, the ideal life expectancies were changed in the most recent, 2010 update of the Global Burden of Disease studies. Currently, ideal life expectancy at birth is 86 years both for men and women. There is no longer a difference in the burden of premature death between the sexes. The change also reflects the gains in life expectancy in the last couple of decades – in Japan, life expectancy at birth for women has reached 85.9 years – as well as the gradual narrowing of the life expectancy gap between men and women.

After this small detour, let us continue with the calculation of years of life lost. On the current methodology, if a person dies at 50, the years of life lost are just over 37 years. This represents the burden of premature mortality associated with this person's disease or injury. (Of course,

50 plus 37 is more than 86. But there is no error in the math here: the years of life lost are greater than the 36 you might expect, because average life expectancy at birth and average life expectancy at 50 are different. If you survive to 50, you can expect to live longer than you could expect to live at birth. The average increases because some people in your birth cohort have already died. If you survive to 80, your ideal life expectancy is another 11 years.)

The other component of DALYs is years of life lived with disability, used to represent non-fatal health outcomes. If a person has diabetes or if she is blind, her health-related quality of life falls short of perfect health. Each year she spends having the condition is adjusted for her health-related quality of life, just as in the case of QALYs. The *disability weights* that are used in DALYs represent the burden of the disability associated with particular diseases and injuries. (Recall that disabilities are losses of ability to carry out normal human activities.)

The latest version of the Global Burden of Disease studies includes almost three hundred different diseases and injuries. These are the *causes* that lead to particular pathological conditions. These pathological conditions are called *sequelae*, and the latest version counts well over a thousand of them. They include such diverse conditions as anemia due to malaria, heart failure due to ischemic heart disease, measles, major depressive disorders, and so on. In many cases, the treated and untreated forms of a disease are also distinguished. AIDS with antiretroviral treatment is treated as a separate condition from AIDS without antiretroviral treatment. In other cases, the phases of a condition are also distinguished: a cancer can be controlled, metastatic, or in the terminal phase.

Not all of these conditions need to be assigned a separate disability weight, however, since multiple conditions can lead to the same health outcome. For instance, anemia can have a genetic cause or it be caused by vitamin deficiency, iron deficiency, by certain chronic or infectious diseases, and so on. Anemia due to malaria is a separate condition from anemia due to maternal hemorrhaging, or anemia due to peptic ulcer disease. But all of these conditions can be given a common disability weight insofar as they lead to very similar health outcomes. Thus, the Global Burden of Disease study associates the over one thousand conditions with 220 different health outcomes. The health outcomes represent the disabilities that result from the pathological conditions – which can be caused by roughly three hundred different diseases and injuries.

This might sound more complicated than it is. In a nutshell, the idea is to identify the diseases and conditions that are the ultimate causes of many pathological conditions, and then associate all these conditions with the 220 health states that represent similar levels of disability. In the final step, these disabilities are assigned weights that represent their burden.

Thus, the disability weights express lost health-related quality of life. They are measured on a scale between 0 and 1. Compared to QALYs, the scale, however, is inverted: full health is represented by 0, death is represented by 1, and disabilities are represented by weights between 0 and 1. The smaller the weight, the smaller the burden of the disability. This is because DALYs represent harm: the greater the disability weight, the greater the harm.

For an example, consider anemia again. It can have several different causes, and it is associated with several conditions. But in terms of health-related quality of life, what matters is the resultant disability. Evidently, however, anemia can cause different levels of disability. So anemia comes with mild, moderate, and severe forms. The disability weight of mild anemia is 0.005; the weight of moderate anemia is 0.058; and the weight of severe anemia is 0.164.

Here are some other examples of disability weights: AIDS without antiretroviral treatment has a disability weight of 0.547; severe dementia has 0.438; uncontrolled asthma 0.132. Acute schizophrenia has a disability weight of 0.756.

DALYs are the sum of years of life lost due to disability and the years of life lived with disability. The burden of the years of life lived with disability is determined by the disability weights. For example, suppose that a person at 40 is struck by a disease whose disability weight is 0.5 and which kills him at age 50. The burden of this condition is 37 years of life lost, as well as ten years of life spent with a disability whose weight is 0.5. Altogether, these are about 42 DALYs (0.5×10 and the years of life lost due to death at 50). This is the burden of this person's disease. Since this is a harm, the smaller this number is, the smaller the burden.

Therefore, 1 DALY can represent one year of lost life, or two years with a disease whose disability weight is 0.5, four years with a disease whose disability weight is 0.25, and so on. If you add up the burden of disease for each person within a population, you get a summary measure of the overall burden for that population. This can then be compared with similar measures for other countries or regions of the world.

You can also examine the burden of disease globally, according to different causes – tracing back the DALYs associated with different conditions to the diseases and injuries that are responsible for them. According to 2010 data, the top causes of the global burden of disease are ischemic heart disease, followed by lower respiratory infections, stroke, diarrhea, and HIV/AIDS. The list continues with lower back pain and malaria. Notice that not all of these are important causes of mortality. Lower back pain, for instance, has a great health burden, but it is negligible as a cause of death. Lung cancer is a major cause of premature mortality, but because of the high average age of death and the low number of years lived with disability associated with it, it is not a major cause of the overall burden of disease. Ischemic heart disease, lower respiratory infections, and stroke, however, are important causes both of premature mortality and the overall burden of disease.

The data can also show changes over time. In 2004, the top five leading causes of the burden of disease worldwide were lower respiratory infections (94.5 million DALYs), diarrheal diseases (72.8 million DALYs), unipolar depressive disorders (65.5 million DALYs), ischemic heart disease (62.6 million DALYs), and HIV/AIDS (58.5 million DALYs). In recent years, an increasing proportion of the global disease burden is attributable to chronic disease compared to infectious disease, and this trend is expected to continue. .

Furthermore, there continue to be enormous variations between different countries and regions of the world. In high-income countries, the causes of the burden of disease in 2004 were unipolar depressive disorders (10 million DALYs), ischemic heart disease (7.7 million DALYs), and cerebrovascular disease (4.8 million DALYs). At the same time, in low-income countries, the leading causes were lower respiratory infections (76.9 million DALYs), diarrheal diseases (59.2 million DALYs), and HIV/AIDS (42.9 million DALYs). Note the difference between the magnitude of these numbers in the two groups of countries. Finally, there are enormous variations in the distribution of the burden of disease between age groups. According to the 2004 study, 36 percent of the total disease burden in the world falls on children under 15 years – almost all of them living in low- and middle-income countries.

Originally, when the Global Burden of Disease project began in the early 1990s, the disability weights were determined on the basis of studies with various trade-off questions, using groups of health care professionals from different countries as respondents. The developers of the DALY argued that health care professionals are the best placed to determine disability weights, since they are the most familiar with a wide range of health conditions. This procedure has received a lot of criticism.

One of the objections was that it is unlikely that the weights determined by health care professionals have any inter-cultural validity. Disabilities, it was argued, come with different burdens in different social and cultural settings. It is unlikely, therefore, that it is possible to assign the same weight to the same disability in different settings. The measurement of DALYs, therefore, lacks inter-cultural validity.

In response, disability weights were re-estimated for the 2010 update of the Global Burden of Disease studies. Instead of health care professionals, general population samples were used. The researchers undertook two kinds of surveys. In the first one, household surveys were carried out in five different countries. They interviewed almost thirteen thousand individuals in Bangladesh, Indonesia, Peru, Tanzania, and the United States. The second survey was web-based. Anyone could take part in it. Overall, almost thirty thousand respondents helped evaluate the burden of particular disabilities on the basis of pairwise comparisons of health states.

The most important finding of the surveys was a high degree of agreement in the responses. Respondents from very different social, economic, and cultural backgrounds gave very similar evaluations. The high degree of agreement serves as evidence that DALYs can be applied in different settings. People from different backgrounds largely agree on the badness of different health conditions.

Nevertheless, the new surveys did not address another objection. According to some critics, the badness of different conditions should be evaluated only by those who are the most familiar with those conditions: the patients.

2.5 Whom to ask?

One unresolved issue in health-related quality of life measurement concerns the role of the respondents whose evaluations are used to determine the quality-adjustment factors in QALYs and other health-related quality of life measures. Normally, quality of life researchers use a random sample of respondents. In the United Kingdom, for instance, responses to the EQ-5D questionnaire from samples of the general population have been used to evaluate new interventions and health care services.

The disadvantage of this approach is that it is unlikely that everyone can evaluate different health states equally well. Some people are more familiar with a given health state than others. They have experience of it, or know someone who has experienced it. This was one of the reasons the developers of DALYs originally used responses from health care professionals to assign disability weights. Health care professionals are more familiar with diseases and injuries than members of the general public. They know better what it is like to live with them.

But the best knowledge might be the patients' knowledge. After all, they have first-hand experience of what it is like to live with a condition. In fact, many health-related quality of life questionnaires are designed for patients, especially those that are concerned with the treatment outcomes associated with particular conditions. But general measures (like QALYs and DALYs) seldom use patient evaluations.

One reason for this is practical. If health states were evaluated only by those who have experience of them, different groups of respondents would have to be used for each of them. This would be prohibitively expensive. But there is also a deeper problem here. People who have a chronic illness or permanent functional limitation often *adapt* to their condition: they cope with it by changing their aims, adjusting their plans, and learning new ways to live with their limitations. Adaptation means that often, though not always, they judge their own health state as *less bad* than others. (Some forms of mental illness are exceptions. It is impossible to adapt to unipolar major depression.) In general, health professionals and family members of people living with a particular condition rate that condition worse than the people who themselves have the condition, and members of the general public rate it even worse than health professionals and family members.

Adaptation is another manifestation of the inseparability problem. When people living with a condition judge their health less bad than others, their evaluation is influenced by other factors. Their lower health-related quality of life does not necessarily lead to proportionally lower overall well-being, because they are able to compensate for their health limitations within other components of well-being. But people who do not have experience of the condition disregard the possibility of successful adaptation.

The discrepancy between the evaluations of patients and the general public leads to a paradox. On the one hand, if the values of patients who have successfully adapted to their condition are used, then the quality-adjustment factors will be higher – the health state turns out to be *less bad*. That means that its prevention, treatment, and rehabilitation will be considered less urgent. It will have lower priority in the allocation of health care resources.

On the other hand, if the values of the general public are used in determining the health-related quality of life associated with particular conditions, their prevention and treatment will be more urgent, because of the lower quality-adjustment factor that results from the responses of people less familiar with those conditions. But it would be a bit peculiar to say that less-informed respondents have a more accurate view on the urgency of the prevention and treatment of disability and chronic disease.

Some people believe it is self-evident that the values of patients should be used. They know more about their conditions. They know it is possible to adapt to them and to lead happy and successful lives. But you have to be careful with this argument: adaptation is not always desirable or admirable. You can adapt to limitations by finding other worthwhile goals and activities. But you can also adapt to limitations by giving up your goals and activities and learning to be content with less. Adaptation is not always a healthy way to cope with adverse circumstances.

One solution to this problem may be to use a *deliberative process* in health state evaluation. Some health economists have suggested that respondents should be given a chance to discuss, reflect on, and even revise their evaluations in the light of further information and discussion with patients. This could lead to more agreement on quality adjustment factors, and allow respondents to consider whether adaptation is desirable in particular cases.

Others have argued that health care resource allocation concerns the choices that particular societies make about the use of scarce common resources. These choices should reflect the values of the general population, rather than particular patient groups. Some also add that we should worry less about funding treatments that should not be funded and more about *not* funding treatments that should be. Therefore, when in doubt, you should use the lowest quality-adjustment factors. You should, that is, err on the side of caution.

As this very brief survey shows, there is no generally accepted solution to this problem.

Chapter summary

In order to allocate health care resources fairly and efficiently, we need to be able to measure the value of health: its contribution to quality of life. Although the impact of health on quality of life is difficult to separate from the impact of other components of quality of life, researchers have developed a number of methods for measuring health-related quality of life. These are typically based on surveys for describing and evaluating different health states. On the basis of these evaluations, it is possible to construct general measures of health-related quality of life, including quality-adjusted life years (QALYs) and disability-adjusted life years (DALYs). This chapter has provided a survey of these procedures. We also presented some of their underlying assumptions as well as some of their problems.

Discussion questions

1. Consider the EQ-5D questionnaire in Figure 2.1 on page 34. In your view, is it capable of adequately describing and distinguishing health states? Why or why not? What questions would you add or remove?

2. We argued in this chapter that the standard gamble and the time trade-off may be more adequate methods for eliciting health state valuations than the rating scale, because patients are sometimes required to make treatment gambles or make trade-offs between health states. Evaluate this argument. Is it relevant to the assessment of different methods?

3. When health-adjusted life expectancies are calculated, it is assumed that each health state has the same value at different ages (that is, the quality-adjustment factors are the same). Do you agree with this assumption?

4. In calculating the burden of disease in a population, you can use either actual life expectancies or some ideal life expectancy for representing the harm of premature mortality. What are the advantages and disadvantages of these alternatives? Which one should be used?
5. Suppose you are trying to determine the burden of a particular health condition. For determining the quality adjustment factor of this condition, you can survey either a sample of the general population or a sample of patients who have had the condition. Which sample should you use? Why?

Further readings

An excellent introduction into health evaluation is the collection by Murray *et al.* (2002). Broome (2002) and Brock (2002*a*) are two discussions of the inseparability problem in that volume. See also Bognar (2008*b*) on this topic. A good discussion of philosophical issues in health-related quality of life measurement is Brock (1993). A lot has been written on health state evaluation methods and the construction of QALYs; see, for instance, Froberg and Kane (1989*a,b,c,d*) or Weinstein *et al.* (2009). For philosophical assessments and arguments, see Broome (1999*b*), Hausman (2006), and Nord *et al.* (2009). (The last paper reports the study on the comparison of values of health states obtained by the rating scale, standard gamble, and time trade-off methods.) For DALYs and the Global Burden of Disease Project, see Murray (1996) – this is now, however, outdated with the publication of the 2010 Update, which introduced a number of methodological and philosophical revisions. (For the update, see the articles in *The Lancet* 380(9859) [December 15, 2012] issue, also available at http://www.thelancet.com/themed/global-burden-of-disease.) For the problem of adaptation, see Menzel *et al.* (2002) and Wolff *et al.* (2012).

Note

1 Preamble to the Constitution of the World Health Organization, 1946, available at http://apps. who.int/gb/bd/PDF/bd47/EN/constitution-en.pdf.

3 Ethics and cost-effectiveness

3.1 What is cost-effectiveness analysis?

In the previous chapter, we looked at the measurement of the value of health. As we explained, you need to measure the value of health if you want to know how much different interventions and health care services benefit people. But in order to fully evaluate them, this is only one side of what you need to know. You also need to know their cost.

Cost-effectiveness analysis (CEA) is a tool for evaluating the overall health benefits of interventions and health care services, taking account of their costs. It works by comparing the ratios of their costs and benefits, and by ranking them on this basis. The lower the ratio, the more cost-effective they are.

Let us begin with an example. Suppose you are presented with a number of alternative programs for saving the lives of patients with a terminal illness. Program 1 and Program 2 would both cost $10 million. But Program 1 would save the lives of 100 patients, whereas Program 2 would save the lives of only 80 patients. It is easy to see the advantage of Program 1: by choosing this program, you can save one life for $100,000, whereas on Program 2, you can save one life for $125,000. Thus, Program 1 enables you to save more lives for less per person.

The cost-effectiveness of an intervention is given by the simple formula

$$CEA \ ratio = \frac{cost}{unit \ of \ benefit}$$

In our example, the unit of benefit is a saved life, and the cost is $10 million. Other things being equal, the smaller this ratio, the better. Since Program 1 saves more lives for the same cost, it has a more favorable cost-effectiveness ratio than Program 2.

Consider Program 3 now. On this program, you can save 110 people. But this program is more expensive: it would cost $12,100,000. This means that you have to spend $110,000 for each life you save. Therefore, even though Program 1 would save fewer lives than Program 3, it is more cost-effective.

Suppose your goal is to maximize health benefits (we set aside other moral considerations for the moment). In that case, comparing the cost-effectiveness ratios of these programs provides you with a way to rank them: Program 1 is more cost-effective than Programs 2 and 3, and Program 3 is more cost-effective than Program 2. Based on this ranking, you can claim that Program 2 should not be chosen when Program 1 is available. Since Program 1 saves more lives for the same cost, there is no reason to prefer Program 2.

But perhaps you should not prefer Program 1 to Program 3. Even though it costs less, it has a worse outcome – fewer lives saved. In comparing two interventions, it is only some of the time that one intervention is better than another both in terms of its outcome and its costs. Other times, one intervention has an advantage in terms of its outcome, but not in terms of its costs, or in terms of its costs, but not in terms of its outcome.

So, whether Program 1 or Program 3 should be chosen might depend on further factors. For instance, it might depend on the size of your budget. If your budget is limited to $10 million, then Program 1 is definitely better than Program 3. If you chose Program 3 under these circumstances, you would run out of money after saving 90 lives. And even if you have a bigger budget, there might be competing programs that you could not afford if you chose Program 3.

In practice, policymakers are often interested simply in distinguishing between those interventions that are "good value for money," and those that are not. After ordering all interventions in terms of their cost-effectiveness into a *priority list*, they establish a cut-off point on the list. The items ranked above this threshold are considered cost-effective. They are good value for money. Below the threshold, the items are deemed not to be cost-effective. They should have less priority. Thus, when they decide how to spend their budget, policymakers can try to provide as many of the cost-effective interventions as possible. For instance, they might offer them as part of a health insurance package.

It is important to recognize that cost-effectiveness analysis itself does not tell you where the cut-off point should be. That is a matter for society to determine. It is a matter of moral argument. A society, for example, might decide that $100,000 per life saved is the cut-off point above which a program is not considered cost-effective. This is how much this society is willing (or able) to spend on saving lives in the health care system. Given this, Program 1 is (just barely) cost-effective, and Program 3 is not.

It is also important to note that our example is simplified in at least three ways. First, we should point out that this is seldom the right way to compare Program 1 and Program 3. After all, Program 3 would save ten additional people: 110 rather than 100. Usually, what you would be concerned with is not comparing overall costs and benefits, but with how much it would cost to bring about additional benefits.

Suppose your health care system is trying to decide whether to implement Program 1 or Program 3. Remember that Program 1 costs $10 million and saves 100 people for $100,000 each; Program 3 costs $12,100,000 but saves 110 people for $110,000 each. To make a decision, you need to consider the costs of saving ten additional people. Whichever program you choose, you will save 100 people. If you spend an extra $2,100,000 by implementing Program 3, you save ten more people. But the real cost of saving them is not $110,000. It is actually $210,000 – almost twice as much. Program 3 looks much less attractive now.

In real life, health care resource allocation is often about these sorts of comparisons: when is an intervention or health care service an *improvement* over another in terms of its costs and benefits? How much additional benefit would it bring, and at what cost? In other words, what needs to be considered is *incremental cost-effectiveness*: the ratio of an intervention's additional costs to its additional benefits.

Suppose now that you can actually *combine* Program 1 and Program 3. You can implement Program 1, and spend the remaining $2,100,000 on Program 3, saving additional people for $110,000 each. Now you can save nineteen additional people, instead of only ten. This might seem surprising. But remember that Program 1 has already saved 100 people for $100,000 each, so for the additional amount you can save more people for $110,000 each. Combining Program 1 and Program 3 takes you further.

This leads to the second way our example is an oversimplification. Health care resource allocation choices become very complex, very fast. The costs of interventions can often depend on other interventions that are already in place. There is a sense in which costs and benefits interact. If Program 1 is available, Program 3 might be very good value. If it is not available, it is less valuable. In real life, decisions are seldom as uncomplicated as the examples in this book.

Before we introduce the third way our example is simplified, it is worth pausing for a moment to address one objection. Many people are horrified by the ideas that we are introducing in this chapter. "Surely," they might say, "you cannot put a monetary value on saving a person's life. People are not commodities. It is repugnant to even think about how much it is worth to save a person's life."

It should now be clear why this objection is based on a misunderstanding. Cost-effectiveness analysis does not put a monetary value on lives. It does not put a price tag on persons. It is concerned with the value of interventions. Some interventions save lives, but their value is not determined by some calculation of the worth of people. It is determined by the comparative costs and benefits of those interventions. To see this, suppose that you suffer from the condition that Program 1 targets. If it is implemented, your life can be saved for $100,000. Suppose also that I suffer from the condition that Program 3 targets, so my life can be saved for $110,000. Does it follow that my life is more valuable than yours? Surely not. I just happen to suffer from a condition that is more expensive to treat. It would be absurd to conclude that my condition makes my life more (or less) valuable. Yet sadly, many critics continue to complain that cost-effectiveness analysis puts a monetary value on people's lives. They argue it is wrong to think about questions of life and death in terms of costs and benefits.

Of course, it can often be difficult to think about resource allocation choices, since they can have profound consequences. But refusing even to think about their costs and benefits is much worse. How would you know, in that case, that Program 2 should not be chosen if Program 1 is available? How would refusing to consider costs and benefits be a consolation to those whom you cannot save?

Cost-effectiveness analysis is not about putting a price on people's lives or health. It is important to keep this point in mind.

3.2 Calculating health benefits

Here is the third way our example in the previous section was simplified. So far, we have considered costs. Now we will consider benefits.

In the three programs, we used "lives saved" as the unit of benefit: we evaluated them in terms of how many terminally ill patients they would cure. While this served the purposes of illustration, a "life saved" is actually not a very useful unit. For one thing, you cannot literally "save" a person's life: all you can do is to extend the time the person is alive. In our example, we implicitly assumed the time for which our patients would survive would be the same for all of them in all three of the programs. We also assumed they would be equally healthy during this period. We assumed, in other words, that other things were equal.

Evidently, however, it matters crucially how long an intervention can extend a patient's life. Other things being equal, an intervention that extends life by ten years is better than one that extends life by one year only. The "quantity" of life – the overall number of months or years that patients can expect to gain from an intervention – is an important consideration in measuring health benefits.

More importantly, extending life is often not the only concern. Most of the interventions and services provided by health care systems are not about saving lives, but about maintaining or restoring good health. They have outcomes that affect health-related quality of life: they cure a disease or injury, manage a chronic condition, reduce some health risk, and so on. Other interventions result in some combination of life extension and health improvement: they postpone the patient's death and maintain her at some level of health-related quality of life. Cost-effectiveness analysis needs measures of health benefit that take into account both the quality and the quantity of life. It needs a precise scale for evaluating interventions and health care services with very different outcomes.

This is why evaluative measures, like QALYs and DALYs, are so important. They provide a common unit for measuring benefit. As we explained in the previous chapter, both of these measures evaluate health by weighting the time for which a person is in a particular health state by the health-related quality of life associated with that health state. For convenience, both measures treat one year as their unit of time. Each year is weighted with a factor that represents health-related quality of life. The adjustment factors are between 0 and 1: on the QALY scale, full health is represented by 1 and a health state that is no better than death is represented by 0. Hence, if an intervention results in one year in full health, its value is 1 QALY (no adjustment factor). If it results in one year with a poorer health-related quality of life, the value of that year is lower. The closer the values to 1, the better the health-related quality of life.

QALYs provide a straightforward basis on which the effectiveness of interventions and health care services can be evaluated. If an intervention ensures an extra life year at the health-related quality of life level of 0.8, it is more effective than another that results in an extra life year at the level of 0.5. But if the second intervention ensures *two* extra life years at this level, then it is more effective than the first: two years at 0.5 is a better outcome in this respect than one year at 0.8. It results in more QALYs (2 × 0.5). This is how QALYs allow us to combine quality and quantity of life.

Let us return to our initial example. To keep things simple, suppose that all three health programs ensure survival in full health for two years. Saving each person results in exactly 2 QALYs. Thus, Program 1 results in two extra life years for 100 people and thus provides 200 QALYs; Program 2 results in two extra years for 80 people and provides 160 QALYs; and Program 3 results in 220 QALYs. Since now we have a measure of benefit less crude than "lives saved," the programs can be compared in terms of how many QALYs they result in for a unit of cost:

$$CEA \ ratio = \frac{unit \ of \ cost}{QALYs}$$

We can now confirm that Program 2 should indeed not be chosen when Program 1 is available. If, for the sake of simplicity, we set the unit of costs to $100,000, then Program 1 results in 2 QALYs per unit of cost (since it results in 1 QALY for $50,000), and Program 2 results in 1.6 QALYs for each unit of cost (since it results in 1 QALY for $62,500). Programs that result in more QALYs should have, other things being equal, higher priority.

We can also reconsider whether Program 1 should be given priority compared to Program 3. Program 1 extends the lives of 100 people for two years for only $10 million. Program 3 extends the lives of 110 people for the same time, but it costs $12,100,000. We were unsure before how to compare interventions that have better results but require more resources with interventions that have worse results but require fewer resources. We can now calculate that for each unit of cost, Program 3 results in slightly more than 1.8 QALYs. (It results in 1 QALY for $55,000.) Consequently, Program 1, which results in 2 QALYs per unit of cost, is indeed better in this respect than Program 3.

Measuring cost-effectiveness in terms of QALYs greatly simplifies the evaluation of interventions and health care services. You can simply look at how many QALYs are gained by an intervention – or, equivalently, how much it costs for the intervention to create a QALY – regardless of whether the intervention benefits people by extending their lives, improving their health-related quality of life, or some combination of the two. You can also express the value of an intervention that extends life but reduces health-related quality of life, or one that improves health-related quality of life but reduces life expectancy.

In practice, the QALYs associated with an intervention are averages. For example, suppose that cancer Treatment A typically extends the life of patients by five years but it is accompanied by severe limitations in functioning. The health-related quality of life in each of the five years is only 0.4. Treatment B, in contrast, provides a shorter remission but causes less severe functional limitations. Typically, patients on this treatment survive for only three years, and their health-related quality of life is 0.8 in the first year, 0.7 in the second, and 0.6 in the third. Thus, Treatment A results in 2 QALYs per patient, and Treatment B results in 2.1 QALYs. Assuming their costs are equal, Treatment B is more cost-effective.

There is nothing that prevents you from using other outcome measures in cost-effectiveness analysis. With a small modification, you can use DALYs as well. The disability weights in DALYs represent the burden of different diseases and injuries. While QALYs are a measure of health benefit, DALYs are a measure of disease burden. Since DALYs represent harm rather than benefit, their scale is inverted: 1 represents death and 0 represents full health. The lower the disability weight, the less burdensome the condition: a disease with a disability weight of 0.2 is less bad than a disease with a disability weight of 0.5. Life years and disability weights, however, are combined in a similar way that they are in QALYs. If a disease has a disability weight of 0.2, then the burden of a year with that disease is 0.2, the burden of two years is 0.4, and so on. (In practice, the calculation is more complicated, but we can set the complications aside here.) Suppose then that Disease A lasts for five years and has a disability weight of 0.3; Disease B lasts for four years but has a disability weight of 0.4. The burden of Disease B is greater (1.6 DALYs) than the burden of Disease A (1.5 DALYs). Assuming the costs are the same, a health program that targets Disease B results in a greater reduction of the disease burden in the population than a program targeting A.

When DALYs are used in cost-effectiveness analysis, the aim is to minimize the burden per unit of cost. The greater the DALY reduction that can be achieved for each dollar spent, the more cost-effective the intervention. An important goal of health care resource allocation, therefore, is to maximize QALYs or to minimize DALYs.

3.3 How is cost-effectiveness analysis used?

Cost-effectiveness analysis can be used in many ways. At the level of the health care system, it can be used to calculate how much different interventions and health care services reduce morbidity and mortality in the population. Policymakers can use this information to decide which interventions should be provided or should have higher priority. Cost-effectiveness analysis can also be used as a guide for public health policy and for making long-term investments in health: for instance, for deciding where to build a hospital or clinic, or how to organize a screening program.

Other activities that can be evaluated by cost-effectiveness analysis include measures to improve the quality of care, programs for promoting healthy behavior and access to healthy alternatives (for instance, calculating the costs and benefits of anti-smoking campaigns or the iodization of salt), or regulations of risky behavior (for instance, determining whether taxes on alcohol and unhealthy food can be successful in improving population health).

When they decide how to allocate resources for health, all health care systems and health insurance providers consider costs and benefits one way or another. Often, they use cost-effectiveness analysis in some form, although there are differences in how rigorous they are in applying its methodology and how transparent they are about their decision-making. Moreover, cost-effectiveness is almost never the only consideration in health policy. Nevertheless, cost-effectiveness analysis is becoming more and more important as societies are struggling with rising health care costs. In some cases, it has already taken center stage. What follows is a quick tour around the world.

The Oregon Health Plan

In the late 1980s, the government of the state of Oregon in the United States attempted to extend Medicaid coverage to all potentially eligible residents by limiting the number of services that would be covered. (Medicaid is a health care program for low-income individuals and families, funded jointly by the states and the federal government.) The Oregon Health Services Commission was created to develop a priority list of health services. The Commission consisted of five primary care physicians, a public health nurse, a social worker, and four representatives of the public.

Why did Oregon decide that it needs to limit the services covered in its Medicaid program? The country had just emerged from a recession during which deep budget cuts had been made. The state government had tried to cut its budget shortfall by dropping thousands of people from its coverage and cutting back on health care services. When a 7-year-old boy suffering from a form of leukemia died after having been denied funding for a bone-marrow transplant, the public was outraged. But the transplant would have cost $100,000. The government knew that re-instituting funding for the handful of patients whose lives could be saved each year would inevitably mean that other life-saving programs would have to be cut. At the same time, the 400,000 Oregonians who neither had private insurance nor were covered by Medicaid would not have access to any sort of health service, let alone organ transplants.

The state government realized that it had to balance costs, benefits, and access in the face of scarcity of resources. It could try to cover services regardless of their effectiveness and cost, but then it would not be able to provide them to everyone who was eligible for the Medicaid program. Or it could try to extend coverage for everyone who was eligible, but then it would not be able to provide all beneficial services. Either it had to limit the program to the most cost-effective services, or it had to deny health care to many people.

The decision was made to try to cover every eligible resident of the state (those whose family income was below the poverty level defined by the federal government). The priority list, drawn up by the Health Services Commission after extensive consultation with the public, would determine which interventions and health care services were to be covered. The coverage decisions were to be made on the basis of cost-effectiveness analysis. The Commission began by pairing up different conditions with their treatments. In the next step, a cost-effectiveness ratio was calculated for each condition-treatment pair, using QALYs as the measure of health benefit. Finally, all interventions and services were ranked according to their cost/QALY ratio. The final list consisted of 709 condition-treatment pairs.

The aim was to identify the most cost-effective items on the list. These would be covered for every Medicaid patient. Further down the priority list there was a cut-off point, below which the treatments were deemed not worth the costs. These treatments would not be provided. The cut-off point was drawn at item 587. Therefore, the state would cover all items ranked from 1 to 587 to every eligible resident.

Interventions which were not to be covered included liver transplants to treat cirrhosis, treatment for people at the final stages of AIDS, and treatment for extremely low birth weight infants. In contrast, preventive and primary care as well as maternal and child health care services were ranked high on the list. Thus, the prevention of HIV had high priority, but the treatment of AIDS during its final stages did not.

Oregon had to apply for permission by the federal government to implement its plan. But it ran into problems. In 1991, the federal government rejected the plan on the basis that it violates the Americans with Disabilities Act (ADA) by discriminating against people with disabilities. The government pointed out that one of the factors taken into account in the cost-effectiveness ranking was whether a treatment would remove all symptoms. But, it argued, this discriminates against those who cannot be returned to full health – those who remain with functional limitations after treatment. The government insisted that a treatment cannot get low priority simply because, for instance, it leaves a disabled person wheelchair-bound.

Many advocates applauded the decision. A researcher of the United Cerebral Palsy Associations worried that under the Oregon plan "disabled people may not get the services they need when a real individual walks into a real doctor's office."[1] Al Gore, a US Senator, wrote, "health care is about helping people, not making life-and-death decisions by playing with spreadsheets."[2]

In response, the state government revised its priority list, and re-applied for a permission in 1993. Eventually, the permission was granted by the federal government – but only on the condition that the priority list is further revised to avoid discrimination against people with disabilities.

Oregon agreed to disregard whether a treatment restores full health. In doing so, cost-effectiveness considerations were relegated to the backseat. Quality of life after treatment was abandoned as a component in the evaluation of the effectiveness of treatments. The factors that were taken into account for any condition-treatment pair were the cost of avoiding death and the probability of death from the condition. Although the

Oregon Health Plan survived, cost-effectiveness did not become the driving principle behind its coverage decisions.

In the next chapter, we will evaluate the objection that the use of cost-effectiveness analysis discriminates against people with disabilities.

New Zealand

In 1993, New Zealand also introduced reforms to its publicly funded health care system. The aim was to identify a package of core health services that would be available to everyone, but would not include everything. The government argued that rationing had always taken place in the health care service, but it had done so without oversight or public scrutiny. It was time to acknowledge that there were limits to the health services the country could afford.

The National Advisory Committee on Core Health Services (today, the National Health Committee) was tasked with determining which health services should be considered core services. But rather than simply coming up with a priority list, the Committee has taken a broader approach: in addition to advising the government on the cost-effectiveness of new and existing technologies and interventions, it has also taken into account equity of access, the reduction of health disparities, and meeting the needs of different groups in the population.

Another agency, the Pharmaceutical Management Agency (PHARMAC), is responsible for assessing pharmaceuticals and related products. It decides which pharmaceuticals are funded by the government, determines the level of subsidies for subsidized medicines, negotiates prices, and ensures that spending on pharmaceuticals stays within the budget. It also runs informational campaigns on the best use of medicines. One of the criteria PHARMAC uses for making its decisions is "value for money" – that is, how much health improvement is gained for each dollar spent on a medicine. But it also takes into account the risks and possible side effects of particular pharmaceuticals, their direct costs to patients, and the special health needs of the Maori and other minorities.

PHARMAC evaluates pharmaceuticals by using cost-effectiveness analysis. The benefits are measured in QALYs. The quality adjustment factors were derived from the EQ-5D questionnaire (discussed in the previous chapter) on the basis of a local survey. It was argued that country-specific health-related quality of life weights were necessary because the health state evaluations of the people in New Zealand might differ from those of people in other countries. But PHARMAC also recommends that the health-related quality of life weights obtained by local studies should be compared with the disability weights used in DALYs to make sure they are consistent with the Global Burden of Disease studies.

PHARMAC's decisions are not always uncontroversial. A few years ago, the agency refused to increase funding for a breast cancer drug called Herceptin. It had already covered a nine-week treatment for breast cancer patients; but patient advocacy groups wanted the agency to fund the treatment for 12 months, which was the standard course of treatment in some other countries. PHARMAC argued that the 12-month treatment for the type of breast cancer did not have any additional benefits over the nine-week treatment. It would also cost $20–25 million to provide the longer treatment for the approximately 350 breast cancer patients a year – while the country spent only around $35–40 million a year on all cancer drugs for all cancer patients (the figures are in New Zealand dollars). As the director of PHARMAC pointed out, the agency needs to take into account the needs of all patients and make sure its funds are spent on medicines that provide the greatest benefit. As he put it, "it's not about who can scream the loudest and who can make the most noise."[3]

But apparently it was. Herceptin became an election issue. The opposition promised to extend funding for the 12-month treatment. After winning the election, it quickly fulfilled its promise.

Yet among developed countries, New Zealand remains one of lowest spenders on pharmaceuticals and health care services. Its annual health spending is around $3,000 per person, compared to approximately $8,000 in the United States (2009 data in US dollars). It also has one of the lowest usages of pharmaceuticals in the developed world. But according to the estimates of the World Health Organization, health-adjusted life expectancy – both for men and women, and both at birth and at age 60 – is greater in New Zealand than in the United States.

The National Health Service

In the United Kingdom, health care is provided by the publicly funded National Health Service (NHS). The NHS is actually comprised of separate health care systems for England, Wales, Scotland, and Northern Ireland. In practice, patients are eligible for health care services in all of these systems.

But residents do not in fact have the same access to health care in all areas. In England and Wales, coverage decisions are decentralized and services are organized by regional trusts. This has led to inequalities between different areas, known as the *postcode lottery*. Since primary care trusts make their own decisions about spending and coverage, a patient might not be covered for the same interventions and pharmaceuticals that other primary care trusts provide for people living in their areas. This is especially true of expensive services and pharmaceuticals – like cancer drugs, or treatments for mental health problems. Some trusts used to spend almost three times as much on cancer care than others. In some cases, patients were ineligible for life-saving cancer drugs which others living a few streets away would have been able to get.

To reduce the effects of the postcode lottery, the government set up the National Institute for Clinical Excellence in 1999 – known today as the National Institute for Health and Care Excellence (NICE) – to formulate guidelines for coverage and spending decisions in the English and Welsh health services. NICE carries out assessments of new medical technologies and medicines, makes recommendations for the best treatment of particular health conditions and the management of chronic disease, and issues guidelines for clinical practice.

Its recommendations and guidelines are based on cost-effectiveness analysis. Health benefits are measured in QALYs. But NICE has never undertaken a systematic review of all medical technologies and health services. Rather, its main goal is to assess new interventions and services to determine whether they are more cost-effective than existing ones. Their inclusion is recommended only if their cost-effectiveness ratio is favorable.

In practice, this means that NICE is interested in the *incremental cost-effectiveness* of new technologies and services – whether they are better value for money than the interventions and services already in place. Anything with an incremental cost-effectiveness ratio under £20,000 per QALY is deemed to be cost-effective. Interventions and services whose incremental cost-effectiveness ratio is more than £20,000 per QALY, but less than £30,000 per QALY, can also be recommended. Above the threshold of £30,000 per QALY, however, interventions and services are not considered cost-effective – though NICE allows there might be further considerations in favor of their provision. For instance, exceptions have been made for some cancer drugs that can extend the life of patients with terminal cancer.

Nevertheless, just like in New Zealand, the coverage of expensive cancer drugs (including Herceptin) remains controversial. Such drugs typically extend life by a few months and in some cases they cost substantially more than £30,000 per treatment. Since those few months are not spent in perfect health, a drug that costs, for example, £60,000 *per treatment* would cost much more than £60,000 per QALY. It might cost, for instance, £120,000 per QALY – an enormous expense for the health care system.

Another controversy has been about patients who "top up" their treatment from their own pocket. Earlier, patients who paid for medicines that were not available because of their unfavorable cost-effectiveness ratio used to lose their eligibility for treatment in the National Health Service. After all, the defenders of this policy argued, no terminally ill patient should see her neighbor in the ward getting treated with drugs that she cannot get. It is not unfair to "level down" to avoid such inequalities in care. Others, in contrast, argued that this is unfair toward those who can afford to pay for expensive medicines out-of-pocket without burdening the health care system. Today, topping up is permitted in the NHS, but only if the purchased drugs are administered in a private hospital or clinic. Therefore, the guidelines of NICE do not deny access to any treatment – as opposed to a common misunderstanding about the NHS. Rather, they determine who pays for the treatment.

This example also illustrates a general point that we have made before: most health care rationing is not about rationing care or deciding which interventions to provide or deny. Less dramatically, most health care rationing concerns subsidies, levels of co-payment, reimbursement, and so on.

In order for its decisions to better reflect the values of the public, NICE has also instituted Citizen Councils to deliberate on the ethical and social issues that its guidelines raise. The membership of the councils represents the population. The members are not experts in health care. Over the years, the work of the council has been summarized in reports on various issues. For instance, one issue was whether severity of illness should be taken into account in cost-effectiveness analysis. Another discussion focused on the role of age in priority setting. A third report tried to answer whether the guidelines issued by NICE should aim to improve the health of the whole population – even at the cost of widening the health gap between different socioeconomic groups – or extra resources should be provided for the health needs of the most disadvantaged members of society. This would narrow health inequalities, but it would require some sacrifice in overall population health.

The Citizen Councils recommended that severity of disease should be taken into account in formulating NICE guidelines, but it should not be incorporated in the calculation of QALYs – in other words, it should be taken into account alongside, but not as a part of, cost-effectiveness calculations. With regard to the role of age, there was little consensus: while the council agreed that age can be taken into account when it is an indicator of some risk factor, there was no agreement whether age in itself should be a factor in the allocation of health care resources – for instance, by giving higher priority to interventions that primarily benefit younger people. Similarly, the council was unable to reach a decision about the trade-off between improving overall population health and giving priority to the health needs of the least advantaged members of society.

We will return to all of these issues later in this book.

The Disease Control Priorities Project

From the early 1990s, the World Bank, the World Health Organization, and other institutions and foundations have been supporting the work of the Disease Control Priorities Project. The aim of this project is to carry out cost-effectiveness analyses of interventions that are especially important in developing countries, and thereby provide information for health care resource allocation choices in low- and middle-income countries.

Many of these countries lack the expertise and resources to collect evidence for the evaluation of medical interventions and health care services in their own population. The publications of the Disease Control Priorities Project assist policymakers by collecting and analyzing cost-effectiveness data from around the world.

Cost-effectiveness ratios are calculated using US dollars and DALYs. The Disease Control Priorities Project uses the disability weights that were established for the Global Burden of Disease studies. The DALYs are not age-weighted, and, unlike the Global Burden of Disease studies, the project uses actual life expectancy data in different regions, rather than ideal life expectancy.

Malaria, for instance, has been ranked the eighth most important cause of the burden of disease worldwide. In Africa, however, it remains among the top contributors, despite recent advances in controlling it. The experts working for the Disease Control Priorities Project have evaluated the cost-effectiveness of different drugs, the use of insecticide-treated nets, and the control of the main vector of the disease (mosquito species of the genus *Anopheles*). For example, the cost-effectiveness ratio of using bed nets treated with insecticides is around $10 per DALY averted. This includes the costs of nets and insecticides, as well as the treatment, transportation, and installation of the nets.

3.4 Equity weights

NICE in England and Wales, PHARMAC in New Zealand, and the designers of the Oregon Health Plan all used QALYs as the measure of health benefit in their cost-effectiveness calculations. For each intervention, they determined how much it would cost to provide it and how many QALYs would be gained. Interventions and pharmaceuticals that had more favorable cost-effectiveness ratios were given higher priority in the allocation of health care resources.

This approach ensures that health benefits are maximized in the population, while keeping down the costs. In addition, it does not distinguish between patients with respect to their age, sex, disability status, or any other characteristic. In effect, the approach assumes that each QALY has the same value regardless to whom it accrues. Its only goal is to maximize health benefits.

Because of this feature, cost-effectiveness analysis is often equated with one form of utilitarianism. That form of utilitarianism is *total utilitarianism*, the view that the morally right action is that which maximizes the sum total of well-being (represented by "utilities"). Many people object to utilitarianism as an ethical theory. A common objection is that utilitarian ethical theories are insensitive to the distribution of well-being. For utilitarians, an unequal distribution is just as good as an equal distribution, as long as total utilities are equal. But many people believe that inequality is morally objectionable, especially if an equal distribution would have the same total of utilities.

Usually, the claim that cost-effectiveness analysis is utilitarian is intended as an objection. Just like utilitarianism, cost-effectiveness analysis is insensitive to the distribution of benefits – that is, the distribution of QALYs. If two interventions have the same costs and would result in the same number of QALYs, cost-effectiveness analysis will judge them equally valuable, even if the first intervention would lead to an unequal distribution of health benefits, and the second to an equal distribution. But many people would find the first distribution morally objectionable because of the inequality.

Nevertheless, it is not precise to say that cost-effectiveness analysis is a form of utilitarianism. For one thing, unlike utilitarianism, cost-effectiveness analysis is not a theory of ethics. Rather, it is a tool for evaluating interventions and health care services. Of course, it is true that it can be used to determine which interventions or services would maximize health benefits. So it does have some resemblance to the utilitarian idea of maximizing utility, since it is concerned with maximizing benefit. It is also true that that the first health economists to employ cost-effectiveness analysis came from the utilitarian tradition. But that is mainly a historical accident. As we have emphasized, the maximization of health benefits is usually only one of the factors that are taken into account in the allocation of health care resources.

Consequently, cost-effectiveness analysis does not have to be "utilitarian." It need not be insensitive to the distribution of health benefits. The total amount of QALYs (or any other measure of health benefit) does not have to be the only consideration that it takes into account. In particular, you are not forced to make the assumption that all QALYs have the same value regardless to whom they accrue. If this assumption is dropped, cost-effectiveness analysis can take into account other moral considerations. We now present some examples.

Consider inequalities in mortality first. Such inequalities are present in every society: worse off social groups tend to have lower life expectancies at every age than better off groups. Differences in premature mortality between the best off and the worst off socioeconomic groups have been widening even in developed countries. For instance, the mortality gap in the United Kingdom is now greater than it has been for almost 100 years. Many people would agree that it is unfair if the burden of pre-mature mortality is so unequally distributed between the more advan-taged and the less advantaged members of society. It is unfair if people who are already worse off in other ways also face greater mortality risks throughout their lives.

One proposal to address this issue is to give different weights to the health outcomes of people in different socioeconomic groups. Suppose that poor people (unskilled laborers, for example) can expect to live on average to 70, but rich people (highly educated professionals) can expect to live to 80. At each age, more poor people die from preventable causes than rich people. Moreover, poor people tend to be sick more often and for longer periods.

It is even possible to quantify these differences with the help of QALYs. For instance, suppose that an unskilled laborer can typically expect to spend 55 years in good health, five years at the health-related quality of life level 0.8, another five years at 0.6, and another five years at 0.4. Her *health-adjusted life expectancy* at birth is

$$55 + 5 \times 0.8 + 5 \times 0.6 + 5 \times 0.4$$

which equals 64. Thus, even though her life expectancy at birth is 70 years, her health-adjusted life expectancy is only 64. Now suppose that a highly educated professional can typically expect to spend five years at 0.7 and another five years at 0.5 at the end of her life. Her life expectancy at birth is 80 years, and her health-adjusted life expectancy is 76. Thus, a laborer can expect to "enjoy" 64 QALYs throughout her life, while a professional can expect 76 QALYs.

If you are concerned with the lifetime inequality between better off and worse off socioeconomic groups, you can give more weight to the addi-tional QALYs of the worse off. Interventions and policies that primarily benefit poor people would then be more valuable from a social perspec-tive. This would help reduce the inequalities in life chances.

In practice, many decisions influence health-adjusted life expectancy. For instance, poorer areas might have worse health facilities than more affluent locations, as in the case of the postcode lottery in the UK. Deci-sions about where to build hospitals and clinics can be made with a view to improving access for the worse off. Maternal and early childhood health care also work to narrow the gap later in life between the better off and the worse off.

Perfect equality would require policies that equalize health-adjusted life expectancy for everyone. But it is unlikely that this could be achieved easily. Policies that help increase healthy life expectancy for the worse off would almost certainly reduce overall population health. For instance, you might be able to increase the health-adjusted life expectancy of the worse off to 67 from 64 only if the health-adjusted life expectancy of the better off decreases to 72 from 76. The outcome is more equal, but the overall number of healthy years that people can expect is reduced. So the crucial question becomes: How much overall health should society sacrifice for reducing the social inequality in health? Plainly, answering this question requires moral argument.

Instead of socioeconomic groups, you can try to address differences between groups of patients. You might believe, for example, that it is more important to treat patients who have a more severe illness regardless of how well off they are otherwise. The health care system should give higher priority to those whose health needs are greater, because they would end up in a worse situation if they were left untreated.

Up to a point, standard cost-effectiveness analysis does take into account the severity of illness before treatment. To keep matters simple, suppose there are two equal-sized groups of patients. All of these patients can be restored to full health. But presently the health-related quality of life of the patients in the first group is 0.6, and the health-related quality of life of the patients in the second group is 0.8. Patients in the first group are more severely ill. Since the health-related quality of life of both groups of patients can be restored to 1 (full health), treating one patient in the first group rather than one in the second group results in a greater health improvement – 0.4 as opposed to 0.2. The improvement is twice as great if patients who are initially more severely ill are provided with the treatment. Other things being equal, cost-effectiveness analysis recommends giving higher priority to these patients.

But this is merely a consequence of the fact that more severely ill patients can often be helped more. The improvement they can achieve is often greater simply in virtue of the fact that the treatment starts from a worse initial condition. You might believe that improving the condition of the more severely ill should have independent weight. For instance, if the patients in the first group could only be restored to 0.8, the health improvement for the patients in the two groups would have the same value. But the fact that the patients in the first group cannot be restored to full health should not count against them.

Moreover, a health improvement to the more severely ill might be considered morally more important even if they cannot achieve a greater improvement. This belief might be based on the view that it is morally more important or urgent to help the worse off. Or it might be based on the view that equality is important. Treating those patients who are less severely ill would increase the inequality between the two groups. If the patients in the second group are treated, they will achieve full health, while the patients in the first group will remain at 0.6. This outcome is very unequal. In contrast, if the patients in the first group are treated, their condition will improve from 0.6 to 0.8, while the patients in the second group remain at 0.8. This outcome is equal. Thus, giving more weight to improving the health of those who are more severely ill may be important because it promotes equality.

Yet another worry about standard cost-effectiveness analysis is that it does not adequately distinguish between the value of preventing death and the value of improving health. Suppose there are two patients who are currently at the health-related quality of life level of 0.5. If the first patient is left untreated, she will die; if she is treated, she will remain at her current level. If the second patient is left untreated, she will remain at her current level; if she is treated, she will be restored to full health. Thus, if they are not treated, the loss to the first patient equals the loss to the second patient – or, equivalently, the gain of treating the first patient equals the gain of treating the second patient. For both of the patients, it is 0.5 – since preventing a decrease from 0.5 to 0 (death) in the case of the first patient has the same relative value as providing an increase from 0.5 to 1 (full health) in the case of the second patient. From the perspective of standard cost-effectiveness analysis, these treatments are equally valuable.

But many people would say that it is more important to treat the first patient. Her potential loss – losing her life – is surely worse than not regaining full health. In other words, people believe that preventing death is morally more important than improving quality of life. Preventing death has special value. When Oregon revised its priority list, it considered the probability of preventing death as one of the most important factors in evaluating condition-treatment pairs.

Up to a point, standard cost-effectiveness analysis does take into account the special importance of preventing death. If a patient's death can be averted, the gain includes the health-related quality of life that she would enjoy all of her remaining years. This often outweighs mere health improvements. Thus, normally, treatments that save lives are more valuable. But sometimes life-saving treatments will be less valuable, because the resulting health-related quality of life is very low – for instance, when patients will have to live in extreme pain and with severe functional limitations. From the perspective of cost-effectiveness analysis, such treatments might not be worth their cost. Sometimes the cost-effectiveness of interventions that prevent death is no better than the cost-effectiveness of interventions that merely maintain or improve health.

One way to incorporate these ethical considerations into cost-effectiveness analysis is to give different weights to health improvements at different health-related quality of life levels. A common proposal to do this is to use *equity weights*. The easiest way to explain this proposal is with the help of the simple graphs of Figure 3.1.

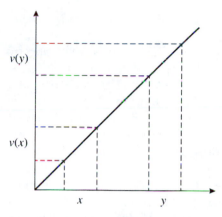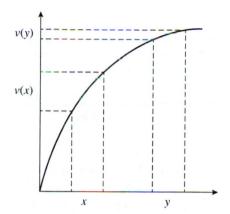

Figure 3.1 Equity weighting.

Consider the left-hand side of the figure first. On the horizontal axis, we represent health-related quality of life. The closer a point to the origin, the worse the health state that it represents. Thus, the interval x represents a health improvement from a very severe initial condition; the interval y represents a health improvement from a much better initial condition. The way the graph is drawn, the magnitudes of improvements x and y are equal.

On the vertical axis, we represent the *moral value* of these improvements. We write $v(x)$ for the value of improvement x, and $v(y)$ for the value of improvement y. The function plotted on the graph – the thick line – expresses the relationship between the *magnitude* of health-related quality of life improvements and the *value* of those improvements.

The left-hand side of the figure illustrates the standard assumption of cost-effectiveness analysis: each unit of improvement has the same value regardless of who receives it. As long as the magnitudes of different health improvements are equal, it does not matter that the patient whose improvement is represented by x is more severely ill than the patient whose health improvement is represented by y. Neither does it matter that treating the second patient would lead to greater inequality. This is because health improvements of the same size have the same value: $v(x) = v(y)$.

The right-hand side of the figure represents a proposal to incorporate equity weights into cost-effectiveness analysis. Here the relationship between the magnitude of health improvements and their moral value is not linear: they increase at a decreasing, but still positive, rate. Health improvements of the same size *do not* have the same value: other things being equal, a given benefit has more value if it goes to those who are more severely ill. Thus, even though the improvements represented by

x and y still have the same magnitude, their value is different. The value of the former is greater: $v(x) > v(y)$.

For the sake of simplicity, our example illustrates equity weighting by considering health-related quality of life improvements only. However, it is straightforward to extend the example to QALYs. The horizontal axis can represent amounts of QALY: the further a point from the origin, the greater the number of QALYs. The vertical axis then represents the moral value of additional QALYs. This way, both health-related quality of life improvements and the duration of improvements are taken into account.

If the QALYs gained from an intervention are weighted this way, a health benefit that goes to a patient who is initially worse off is more valuable than the same benefit to a patient who is better off. The consequence of this in practice is usually that QALYs for the more severely ill are more valuable. Thus, equity weighting can reflect the greater urgency of treating more severely ill patients.

Equity weights also make the value of preventing death more salient. Suppose that the patient whose health improvement was represented by x on the right-hand side of the figure now faces death. Saving her life would extend the magnitude of her health improvement to the origin. Hence, the value of saving her life would be given not by $v(x)$, but $v(x)$ extended to the origin. This makes preventing her death much more valuable than a treatment that results in a health improvement like y (even if it is enlarged by the same amount).

Finally, equity weights work towards reducing inequalities, because they usually imply higher priority to those who are more severely ill and those who would end up worse off. The qualification is needed because marginal health improvements to the more severely ill may not have greater moral value than substantial health improvements to the less severely ill. But normally those who are already worse off and those who would end up worse off if not treated will get priority, leading to more equal health outcomes in the population.

The left-hand side of the figure resembles the way utilitarianism evaluates benefits. For utilitarians, all benefits have the same value. In this respect, standard cost-effectiveness analysis does indeed resemble utilitarianism. The right-hand side of the figure, in contrast, assigns different weights to benefits. It resembles the moral view known as *prioritarianism*. This is, roughly, the view that benefiting a person matters more the worse off that person is. Equity weighting can be interpreted as an application of the prioritarian moral view to health care resource allocation. In Chapter 5, we will give a more complete characterization of prioritarianism. For now, what is important to note is that the weighting of QALYs is an ethical issue — even when weighting is rejected. For the assumption that all QALYs have the same value, regardless of their distribution, rests just as much on an ethical idea as the assumption that QALYs have greater value if they go to the worse off.

Equity weighting can also have a broader interpretation than prioritarianism. The weights can be considered to reflect broader social and moral values that should be taken into account in health care resource allocation. They may represent society's willingness to sacrifice some efficiency gains for greater equality, the importance of meeting needs, the urgency of preventing death, or some other factor. Economists call the choices that take into account these values *equity-efficiency trade-offs*, where "equity" is a catch-all term for all sorts of moral considerations. They are trade-offs because benefit maximization remains an important objective, but other considerations are also given a role.

Benefit maximization remains an important objective because the size of improvements still matters: a sufficiently greater improvement to a less severely ill patient has more value. Just how much greater such an improvement must be to outweigh the benefit to the worse off depends on the shape of the function that is plotted on the right-hand side of the figure. Steeper functions will give less weight to equality and to improving the condition of the worse off. Therefore, the shape of the function expresses the kind of equity-efficiency trade-offs that society is willing (or should be willing) to accept.

Although equity weighting is proposed from time to time, it is seldom used in practice. PHARMAC in New Zealand and NICE in England and Wales do not include equity weights in their cost-effectiveness calculations. The health economists at PHARMAC, for instance, argue that equity weighting should be avoided to keep cost-effectiveness analysis "value-free." Of course, by treating all QALYs as having equal value, they do not keep their cost-effectiveness calculations value-free: they simply use one set of values rather than another. As we have stressed, the assumption that all QALYs have the same value is a value judgment. It is a mistake to think that standard cost-effectiveness analysis does not incorporate moral values.

To be sure, PHARMAC argues that other ethical considerations should be taken into account not as inputs into cost-effectiveness analysis, but alongside it. That is, PHARMAC rejects the use of numerical values to represent these considerations. They are taken into account informally. Similarly, a Citizen Council meeting recommended that NICE should take severity of illness into account – but not in the calculation of QALYs. It should be taken into account as an additional factor. The members of the Council argued that equity weights would make the calculation of QALYs and cost-effectiveness ratios more complicated and difficult to understand.

Equity weighting undoubtedly makes cost-effectiveness analysis more complicated. But refusing to quantify the trade-offs between different

values comes with its own price. On the one hand, cost-effectiveness calculations that only reflect "efficiency" – that is, overall QALY gains and
costs – are doubtless easier to understand. On the other hand, refusing to
make explicit the precise magnitude of the equity-efficiency trade-offs
decreases transparency. It makes it harder to clarify the nature of the
trade-offs and to monitor whether resource allocation choices achieve
ethical objectives. Explicit equity weights could increase the accountability of the health care system.

Admittedly, equity weights might not be able to capture all ethical
considerations. So even with equity weights, cost-effectiveness analysis
should not be the only factor in health care resource allocation. But some
critics go further: they argue that the use of cost-effectiveness analysis will
inevitably lead to unfair discrimination against some patient groups. They
raise fundamental objections to it. If they are right, cost-effectiveness
analysis should not be used at all. We will address these objections in the
next chapter.

3.5 Discounting

Each one of us regularly makes choices that concern the further future. We
make trade-offs between present and future consumption: how much of our
income should we save for later, and how much of it should we spend now?
Should we start exercising now for the sake of a slimmer waistline next
year? How much should we set aside for our retirement years?

People tend to prefer more immediate benefits. This applies to health
just as much as it applies to other goods. People enjoy activities that pose
some risk to their health, they find it difficult to change unhealthy lifestyles, and they often postpone unpleasant experiences, such as visits to the
dentist. They tend to give more weight to more immediate benefits than to
later ones, and less weight to future harms than to more immediate harms.
In the language of economics, they *discount* future harms and benefits.

Some forms of discounting the future are innocuous. Because it is in
the future, a benefit might be more uncertain. Often, it is not irrational
to prefer a certain benefit in the present to an uncertain benefit in the
future, even if the future benefit is greater. Similarly, it is not always
irrational to take a risk of greater future harm to avoid a smaller present
harm. A lot of things can happen between now and the time the harm
might present itself.

There is also a case for valuing monetary benefits more the earlier you
receive them. A dollar that you have today is more valuable than a dollar
that you will have in a year, since you are able to use it immediately.
Discounting commodities that are bought and sold is also uncontroversial. Simplifying greatly, if you can invest your money at a positive

rate of return, you will be able to buy more of a commodity next year. The present value of a commodity exceeds the *present* value of consuming that commodity one year from now. Its value is discounted. Given certain assumptions about the economy, it is not irrational to assign a smaller value to future consumption than to present consumption.

What is more controversial is giving greater weight to present benefits and smaller weight to future harms beyond what would be warranted by considerations of uncertainty and economic factors. Most people seem to have *pure time preferences* – a form of bias for the present. This seems irrational for two reasons. First, pure time preference leads to inconsistency: a person may be willing to forgo a smaller benefit for the sake of a greater benefit tomorrow, but unwilling to make the same trade-off when the benefits are further in the future. Second, pure time preference appears to be a form of discounting *well-being*: a person might prefer the same increase of well-being more in the nearer future than in the further future. However, unlike discounting for uncertainty and discounting economic commodities, the discounting of well-being seems problematic. A painful diagnostic procedure today is going to be just as painful tomorrow. Why should it be considered worse *now*?

If you have pure time preferences, you might consider a smaller loss of well-being today worse than a greater loss of well-being a year from now. But this is puzzling: since the later loss is greater, you should consider it worse. The value of gains and losses of well-being should not vary merely because of time.

This problem arises on the social level as well. In cost-effectiveness analysis, it is customary to discount the future value of interventions. NICE in England and Wales uses a 3.5 percent discount rate in calculating cost-effectiveness ratios. DALYs used to be discounted at a rate of 3 percent both in the Global Burden of Disease studies and in the Disease Control Priorities Project.

Just like in the case of individuals, discounting for uncertainty is uncontroversial in policy. If there is a risk that the benefits of a health program will not materialize, it is rational to take this account. For instance, when research funds are allocated, the benefits of different medical or public health research projects might be highly uncertain. If a research project could potentially lead to great health benefits but has a small chance of success, it might be justified to give it lower priority.

The problem that arises with discounting in cost-effectiveness calculations is that cost-effectiveness ratios combine monetary resources and health benefits. They divide the costs of an intervention with its benefits expressed in QALYs, DALYs, or some other measure. It is customary to discount both the costs in the numerator and the benefits in the denominator. Many philosophers have pointed out that whereas there can be good reasons to discount costs, it is problematic to discount health benefits. Surely, they argue, a QALY today is just as valuable as a QALY tomorrow. Just like in the case of individual time preference, discounting health benefits looks like a pure time preference on the social level, with the added difference that it is not only irrational, but also unethical.

In reply, the defenders of the practice point out that refusing to discount health benefits in cost-effectiveness calculations leads to paradoxical results. Without discounting, it seems rational to use all currently available health care resources for research programs that could lead to the eradication of disease. This is because, in the absence of discounting, the benefits of completely eradicating any disease are extremely great. (Zero incidence till the end of time!) But surely, we should not use all our resources on such programs. We should also spend on controlling disease, improving health, and managing chronic conditions. There are many worthwhile ways to spend our resources.

A compromise position defends discounting by applying a lower rate to the denominator in cost-effectiveness calculations. But even that is problematic. If a lower discount rate was used for health benefits than for costs, it seems that policymakers have a reason to perpetually postpone spending on health. Instead, they should invest all the resources allocated for life-saving interventions this year, so that they can be used next year when the returns make it possible to save more lives. But of course next year they should invest the resources again to be able to save even more lives the year after. Resources could always be used more effectively in the future.

Some health economists argue that costs and benefits should be discounted at the same rate to avoid these problems. But other health economists and many philosophers remain unpersuaded. They point to examples that show that any form of discounting is objectionable. For instance, if health benefits are discounted, interventions that have benefits in the more distant future will be less cost-effective. Immunization against Hepatitis B prevents liver cancer later in life. But since its costs have to be borne in the present, it will have lower priority than interventions with more immediate benefits.

The critics of discounting also worry about the unfairness of putting lower value on the quality of life of future generations, which discounting seems to entail. Plainly, it would be morally wrong to poison the environment for our own benefit at the price of worsening the quality of the lives of our descendants. It would be wrong if cost-effectiveness analysis recommended that. So discounting should be rejected, since it implies a lower value for the quality of life of future people.

In reply, the defenders of discounting remind their opponents that the QALYs in cost-effectiveness ratios are assigned to interventions and health programs. They are used to express the health benefits of an intervention compared to the health benefits of other interventions. And interventions and health care services are merely the *means* of maintaining or increasing health-related quality life. When their value is discounted, it is not implied that health benefits further in the future are less valuable. Just as cost-effectiveness analysis does not put price tags on the life and health of people, discounting need not imply that future lives and health are less valuable. Rather, just as you need to make trade-offs between alternative resource uses, you need to make trade-offs between the use of resources now and in the future. Thus, when QALYs are discounted, it is only the *means to well-being* that are discounted, rather than well-being or quality of life itself.

Again, many philosophers remain unpersuaded. And their arguments have had some success: in its most recent update, the Global Burden of Disease project abandoned the discounting of DALYs.

Chapter summary

Cost-effectiveness analysis is the most important tool for assessing interventions and health care services. It works by comparing their costs and their benefits, where the benefits are usually expressed in QALYs or DALYs. In this chapter, we explained how cost-effectiveness analysis works and illustrated its use by several real-life examples. We also identified a number of ethical issues that arise when cost-effectiveness analysis is part of the allocation of health care resources. We presented equity weighting – a method for taking into account additional moral considerations in cost-effectiveness analysis and for expressing trade-offs between different values in a quantifiable form. We closed the chapter by a discussion of the controversy about discounting future costs and benefits.

Discussion questions

1. Health care systems (or health insurance plans) do not provide every possible beneficial treatment and intervention. Should patients who can afford it be able to pay top-up fees to receive the treatments they want, even when others cannot receive those treatments? What are the ethical issues that this raises?
2. The Ministry of Health is considering the introduction of a colon cancer screening test program. There are two kinds of tests. Test 1 can be offered to everyone, and it would prevent 1,000 deaths from colon cancer. Test 2 is more expensive: it can only be offered to half of the population (who would be selected randomly). This test, however, would prevent 1,100 deaths from colon cancer. Which of these tests should the Ministry of Health introduce?

3. In Section 3.3, we quoted Senator Al Gore, who wrote of the Oregon Medicaid reform plan that "health care is about helping people, not making life-and-death decisions by playing with spreadsheets." What do you think he meant? What was his objection to the Oregon reform plan?

4. In the case of Herceptin in New Zealand, patient advocacy groups had a major role in campaigning against PHARMAC's decision. Some critics argued that it is unfair if better organized, highly visible advocacy groups are able to gain advantages in the health care system for the patients they represent. Do you agree with this argument? What are the ethical issues that patient advocacy campaigns raise?

5. Can you think of any health intervention or policy where cost-effectiveness considerations should be completely ignored? What makes these interventions and policies so important that costs and effectiveness are irrelevant?

Further readings

A more technical, comprehensive, but still accessible introduction to cost-effectiveness analysis is Gold *et al.* (1996). Menzel (1990) and Bell and Mendus (1988) are early discussions of many of the ethical issues discussed in this chapter; more recent discussions are Nord (1999), Ubel (2000), and the more technical Nord *et al.* (1999). The Oregon Medicaid reform has been discussed extensively; see, for instance, Hadorn (1991), Eddy (1992), Kitzhaber and Kemmy (1995), and Blumstein (1997). For the case of Herceptin in New Zealand, see Fenton (2010). The role of cost-effectiveness in the work of NICE is explained by Rawlins and Culyer (2004). The NICE Citizens Council reports are available at http://www.nice.org.uk/aboutnice/howwework/citizenscouncil/reports.jsp.   The work of the Disease Control Priorities Project is presented in Jamison *et al.* (2006); see also their ongoing work at http://www.dcp-3.org. Influential discussions of equity weighting are Wagstaff (1991), Nord (1993), and Williams (1997); for a review of empirical research on equity weights, see Shah (2009). The best discussion of discounting is Broome (1994). The example in Discussion question 2 is taken straight from Ubel *et al.* (1996) – it is worth checking out their survey results!

Notes

1 Quoted in "U.S. Backs Oregon's Health Plan for Covering All Poor People," *The New York Times*, March 20, 1993.
2 Gore (1990, p. 635).
3 Quoted in "Opposition Politicians Criticise Herceptin Decision," *The New Zealand Herald*, August 8, 2008.

4   Problems of discrimination

4.1 Two lines of attack

As we explained in the previous chapter, cost-effectiveness analysis is a tool for evaluating the overall health benefits of interventions and health care services. Each intervention is assigned a cost-effectiveness ratio, with its costs in the numerator, and a measure of the health benefits in the denominator. The lower this ratio, the more cost-effective the intervention. One important principle of the ethics of allocating health care resources is to select the most cost-effective interventions and services.

The measure of the health benefits in the denominator – the "effectiveness" part of the cost-effectiveness ratio – is a combination of two components. The first component is health-related quality of life: the impact of an intervention on the well-being of patients. The more an intervention improves health-related quality of life, the more effective it is. The quality-adjustment factors in QALYs and DALYs are measures of this component. In QALYs, they represent the value of health states. In DALYs, they represent the burden of different conditions.

The second component is the duration of the effect of the intervention. An intervention that has longer-lasting beneficial effects is more effective than one that leads to a shorter improvement. This duration is typically measured in life years. Thus, 1 QALY can represent one year of life in full health, or two years in a health state whose quality-adjustment factor is 0.5, or four years at 0.25, and so on. A QALY is a combination of health-related quality of life and life years. A DALY is a combination of the burden of a disease with the time for which it burdens a person. By calculating the cost/QALY (or cost/DALY) ratio, you can determine how much it costs for any intervention to produce one unit of health improvement.

Both of these components have provided a line of attack to opponents of cost-effectiveness analysis. Some critics have argued that the use of quality of life information leads to unfair discrimination against people with disabilities. Others have pointed out that life years should be considered to have different values at different ages. The duration of the effect of an intervention should count differently depending on how old patients are.

In this chapter, we examine both lines of attack. We first take up the disability discrimination objection, and then turn to the role of age. We conclude by addressing some further moral considerations that cost-effectiveness analysis should take into account.

4.2 Disability discrimination

Some people object to cost-effectiveness analysis because they believe its use unfairly disadvantages certain groups of patients. Since one component of representing the benefits in the cost-effectiveness ratio of an intervention is the health-related quality of life improvement associated with that intervention, patients whose health-related quality of life improvement is limited for some reason will be disadvantaged. In short, patients who have a limited capacity to benefit from an intervention will be discriminated against.

In particular, this will be true of people with disabilities – people who suffer from a permanent functional limitation or from an incurable, but manageable chronic condition. Notice how broad this characterization of disability is. It includes not only blindness or paraplegia, but also diabetes, asthma or allergies. The Americans with Disabilities Act (ADA), for instance, defines disabilities in this broad way, considering a disability any physical or mental impairment that substantially limits major life activities. Critics who object to cost-effectiveness analysis worry that people with disabilities will be discriminated against in health care resource allocation. On this conception of disability, this will include a great number of patients.

We shall call their worry the *disability discrimination objection*. It claims that using cost-effectiveness analysis for allocating health care resources leads to unfair discrimination against people with disabilities. It discriminates against them because it leads to their unequal treatment. Of course, not all forms of unequal treatment are objectionable. (You treat friends and strangers differently.) But the objection claims that in this case the discrimination is unjustifiable. The unequal treatment of people with disabilities is unfair.

Nevertheless, it is not immediately clear what the unfairness consists in. It takes some time to clarify the disability discrimination objection. One difficulty is that it is often formulated in vague terms. Here is a representative formulation:

> A severely disabled person will have a much lower QALY ranking than a person in full health and therefore each year they live will have a lower

(normative) quality of life ranking. But does this mean that the former person's life is less worth living than the latter's; is it thus *worth less*? This goes against a profound belief, both spiritual and secular, that all lives are equally valuable.[1]

Here, the objection is put in terms of QALYs. The claim is that the use of QALYs conflicts with some widely and deeply held moral belief about the value of life. As we will show, there are several ways to understand this claim. We shall argue that they all involve confusion about the idea of the value of a life.

The objection points out that if you represent a person's health-related quality of life by QALYs, a person with a disability will have a lower health-related quality of life than a person in full health. This entails, for instance, that – other things being equal – a person who has difficulties moving around has a worse life than a person with full mobility. Note the importance of the "other things being equal" clause. No one holds that a person who has difficulties moving around must have a worse life *all things considered*.

So, the claim that a person with a disability has a lower health-related quality of life should not be especially controversial. People want to be free of limitations in mobility and in other functions. They hope medicine can help them avoid disabling conditions and trust the health care system to improve their health-related quality of life once they have them. They want and hope these things because, other things being equal, disabilities make life worse.

But as we discussed in Chapter 2, it is also true that people tend to learn to cope with and adapt to their disabilities, and, *all things considered*, they can lead a life that is just as good as the life of anyone else. They can do this because health is only one component of well-being, and its limitations can be compensated by other components of well-being. A person's overall quality of life may be high even though her health-related quality of life is not.

Consequently, it does not follow that a person with lower QALYs will have a worse life, all things considered, than a person in full health. She may or she may not. How much her life is worth living is not only a matter of her health-related quality of life. No one measures the worth of people's lives only on the basis of their health-related quality of life.

But suppose that other things *are* equal. Suppose the lives of two people are identical in every respect, except that one has to live with a disability. Does it follow then that the life of the person with the disability is worth less? No, it does not. For one thing, there is a crucial ambiguity in the objection. It confuses people with their quality of life. There is indeed a profound – and correct – belief that each *person* is equally valuable. There are many ways this belief is expressed in our moral thinking. Each person is entitled to the same set of basic human rights. Each person is owed equal concern and respect. All people's interests should be considered equally. No one should be used as a mere means to the aims of others. Irrelevant characteristics, like race, ethnicity, or sexual orientation do not justify bias or discrimination.

But even though each person has equal worth, not all lives are equally valuable – in the sense that they do not go equally well. A life full of hatred, envy, and loneliness is likely to be less good than a life of empathy, sharing, and deep personal relationships. A life of abject poverty and suffering is worse than a life of good health and a decent standard of living. Common-sense morality makes a straightforward distinction between the *value of persons* and the *quality of their life*. The formulation of the discrimination objection in the quote above reveals a conflation of the two. The use of QALYs does not conflict with the belief in the fundamental equality of persons.

There is also another confusion in the objection. It is in the premise that "a severely disabled person will have a much lower QALY ranking than a person in full health." This is a misunderstanding. Cost-effectiveness analysis does not rank people in terms of QALYs at all. It ranks *interventions*. QALYs are not assigned to patients. They are assigned to the outcomes of treatments, health care services, pharmaceuticals, medical technologies, and so on. In short, the objection confuses selecting treatments with selecting patients.

Consider some of the examples from the previous chapter. In the Oregon Medicaid reform, cost-effectiveness analysis was used to rank condition-treatment pairs. QALYs were assigned to the improvements associated with different treatments, not to individual patients or groups. The controversy over Herceptin in New Zealand was not about a choice between different patient groups, but about a choice between two different courses of treatment for the same patients. In England and Wales, NICE does not make decisions about which patients to treat or whose life is more valuable; rather, it evaluates new medical technologies, interventions, pharmaceuticals, and so on.

When the Oregon Health Plan was initially rejected by the federal government, a researcher of the United Cerebral Palsy Associations applauded the decision because of fears that "disabled people may not get the services they need when a real individual walks into a real doctor's office."[2] But this certainly would not have been the consequence of the reform. What he had in mind, perhaps, was that if an otherwise healthy person and a disabled person had the same medical need, doctors would be required to treat the otherwise healthy person first. In fact, however, there was no such requirement or recommendation in the proposed reform at all. The aim of the reform was to *broaden* access so that all eligible residents of the state would be covered by Medicaid, many of whom had unmet health needs due to disabilities and chronic health conditions.

It is true that one kind of rationing is *triage* – a practice originating from the battlefields of World War I. Faced with the mass casualties of war, doctors separated the injured into three groups: those who were likely to live regardless of the care they would get; those who were likely to die regardless of the care they would get; and those whose life could be saved only if they got immediate care. Priority was given to the patients in the last group. While triage is still used in battlefield medicine and during emergency situations and mass casualty incidents, it is uncommon in everyday medical practice. Ordinary health care institutions rarely face the extreme scarcity of time or personnel that justifies selection between individual patients. The researcher of the United Cerebral Palsy Associations might have thought that cost-effectiveness analysis was about extending triage to all of health care. If he did, he was quite mistaken.

Other things being equal, cost-effectiveness analysis recommends that you give priority to treatments that achieve the greatest improvement in health-related quality of life. Rather than discriminating against those who have low health-related quality of life, it tends to favor their treatment, for the simple reason that the lower a person's health-related quality of life, the more it might be possible to help her. Suppose there are two treatments, targeting different conditions. The first treatment restores the health of patients suffering from a severe condition that leads to low health-related quality of life. The second treatment restores the health of patients who have a mild condition and hence higher health-related quality of life. If other things are equal, the first treatment is more cost-effective. Cost-effectiveness analysis would recommend giving priority to patients suffering from the first condition.

In reply, opponents of the use of cost-effectiveness analysis point out that disabilities and chronic conditions are different. Because of the nature of their condition, patients with disabilities and chronic conditions often cannot be returned to full health. If they have another condition that needs treatment, the health-related quality of life improvement they can achieve is smaller on account of their disability than the improvement that can be achieved by those patients who do not have the disability.

At other times, a disability may reduce life expectancy such that treating patients with the disability produces fewer QALYs. And finally, even if a disabled person could achieve the same health improvement as a patient without disability, the treatment of a disabled person may be more complex, uncertain, or expensive. Therefore, if interventions for disabled people are treated separately in cost-effectiveness analysis, then any of these factors may entail lower priority for treating patients with disabilities. In this indirect way, cost-effectiveness analysis can be used for discriminating between patients. Rather than rationing resources, cost-effectiveness analysis can be used for rationing patients.

The key idea here is that interventions targeting patients with disabilities may be treated separately in cost-effectiveness analysis. This version of the discrimination objection does not claim that the use of cost-effectiveness analysis *necessarily* leads to discrimination against people with disabilities. It claims merely that it may do so if it is used in certain ways – since it can also be used for ranking patients, rather than ranking treatments. Even though there is nothing inherently discriminatory in using cost-effectiveness analysis in health care resource allocation, it does leave open the possibility of unintentional mistakes and intentional abuse.

How serious is this worry in practice? It would plainly be serious if the calculation of cost-effectiveness ratios began from distinguishing between patient groups. However, the way in which QALYs are constructed makes this unlikely. As we explained in Chapter 2, QALY weights are usually based on surveys with questions about the functional limitations that accompany particular conditions. The answers to the questions determine the health state associated with the condition, and that health state is assigned a quality-adjustment factor. Certainly, the survey respondents have different experiences of health. Some of them are likely to have additional disabilities. But when the results are transformed into quality-adjustment factors, such individual differences "wash out." Hence, the QALY gains that get associated with particular treatments represent some average or typical health improvement due to those treatments, ignoring the possible impact of co-disabilities.

Consequently, when a disabled patient and a patient with no disability suffer from the same condition, the doctor will prescribe the same treatment for them. A person in a wheelchair will not get a different treatment or lower priority for treatment. Cost-effectiveness calculations might have been used to decide which treatment should be used for their condition. In such decisions, no patient is considered less worthy of treatment.

Intriguingly, when the federal government rejected Oregon's original submission of its priority list, it did not object to the possibility of using cost-effectiveness analysis to discriminate between different patient groups. It had a different objection. In a letter to the governor of Oregon, the Secretary of Health and Human Services wrote:

> Patient A and Patient B are both injured in an accident. Treatment A is recommended for Patient A, while Treatment B is recommended for Patient B. However, Treatment A will sustain Patient A's life, but will not restore the abilities A lost after the accident (such as an ability to walk), while Treatment B will sustain B's life *and* restore his ability to walk. If the basis for funding B

but not A is a quality-of-life judgment that being able to walk is of greater benefit than not being able to walk, for example, then a decision to deny treatment to A would be discrimination based on A's resulting level of disability. In effect, B's life would be considered more valuable than A's life because B will regain an additional function while A would not. Under the second scenario, a distinction between two effective treatments would be based not on treatment effectiveness, because both treatments would sustain life, but on an inappropriate assessment of the underlying quality-of-life each patient will have after treatment. This scenario describes the Oregon plan.[3]

From a practical perspective, this has proven to be an extremely effective argument. Oregon had to revise its priority list. It was forbidden to take into account cost-effectiveness considerations beyond the cost and probability of preventing death. The argument is also very broad: it denies that health-related quality of life and functional status can ever be taken into account in health care resource allocation. In fact, in the United States, Medicare – the publicly funded health care program for the elderly – is prohibited from considering cost-effectiveness in its recommendations and policies.

Yet it is not entirely clear how to interpret this argument. One of the problems it points to is the quality of life judgment that being unable to walk leads to a lower health-related quality of life. The government seems to deny that being able to walk is a greater benefit than not being able to walk. If so, we suspect this is just another instance of confusing health-related quality of life with overall well-being.

But perhaps the government did indeed intend to deny the underlying health-related quality of life judgment. In that case, however, the objection does not in fact target cost-effectiveness analysis or what Oregon tried to do. Rather, it targets the way health-related quality of life was measured in the Oregon Health Plan. Thus, the government disagreed with a particular quality of life judgment, but not the use of cost-effectiveness analysis. Even so, we suspect that many readers would share our puzzlement about the claim that being able to walk is no greater benefit than being unable to walk.

The point about treatment effectiveness under the "second scenario" is similarly puzzling. The Secretary of Health and Human Services seems to claim that effectiveness has nothing to do with improvement in health-related quality of life. Both treatments in the example should be considered effective, since they sustain life. This is a very impoverished and counterintuitive view of effectiveness. Its flip side seems to be that no treatment that merely improves health is more effective than the next. It does not need spelling out why this is an unacceptable view of effectiveness. We all care about health-related quality of life improvement even when our lives are not at stake.

The argument also suffers from some of the same confusions that we have identified already. It confuses the value of persons with the quality of their lives. It also misunderstands cost-effectiveness rankings. As we have pointed out, Oregon did not try to rank patients. It ranked treatments. It is suggested that Treatment A in the example is less cost-effective than Treatment B, since it does not restore the ability to walk. But it does not follow that Treatment A would not be provided. That depends on where the cost-effectiveness threshold is put in relation to the cost-effectiveness ratios of A and B.

But suppose, for the sake of argument, that Treatment A would be below the threshold. Because of its poor cost-effectiveness ratio, it would not be provided to patients. Even though cost-effectiveness analysis is used only to rank treatments, it can *indirectly* lead to ranking patients. It can lead to the exclusion of those who need treatment A. Whenever a treatment is not provided by the health care system, there will be patients who suffer as a result. Is this a case of unfair discrimination against people with disabilities?

Before the accident, there is no difference between Patient A and Patient B. Right after the accident, the only difference between them is that A would be disabled as a result of treatment. *There is no person with disability before or at the time of the accident.* This case is very much unlike refusing to treat a patient because of their race or sex. It is also very much unlike refusing to treat a patient because they have a preexisting condition. If there is no patient with a preexisting disability, how can this be a case of discrimination against *people with disabilities*?

If the case of A and B is the salient case against cost-effectiveness analysis, then it becomes clear that the objection is much broader. It is not about patients with functional limitations or chronic conditions. The government's real objection appears to be targeted at the use of health-related quality of life information in health care resource allocation in general. It is misleading to put it in terms of disability.

If A is refused treatment, the unequal treatment of A and B in itself is not sufficient to show that A is unfairly discriminated against. Unequal treatment is not necessarily unfair. In the next section, we will consider the view that it is permissible to give different priorities to the treatment of different patients depending on their age. Those who accept this view argue that the unequal treatment of different age groups in the health care system is not unfair. It is not a form of objectionable discrimination.

So, the fundamental question is whether the unequal treatment of A and B is unfair, on the assumption that the treatment that Patient A needs is not cost-effective and therefore not provided. Critics of cost-effectiveness analysis must be able to demonstrate the unfairness.

Perhaps they could reason this way. Each person who needs medical treatment has a moral claim to it. Patients who have the same medical need have equally strong claims. The health care system must meet these needs as much as possible, and it must not differentiate between patients with equal claims. The strength of people's claims might be determined by a number of different factors – the severity of their illness, the probability of death, perhaps their age, or perhaps even whether they are personally responsible for their illness due to their lifestyle choices. But, the argument goes, health-related quality of life after treatment is not one of these factors. How much a patient can benefit from treatment is irrelevant to the strength of her claim. Quality of life is an irrelevant consideration. Taking it into account is unfair.

Is this a good argument? In many health care systems, some forms of treatment for the final stages of terminal cancer are not covered, because they provide very little health-related quality of life improvement for enormous costs. If there was a limitless abundance of resources, it would certainly be morally wrong to fail to provide these treatments. But in conditions of scarcity, not everything can be provided. In such conditions, what is morally wrong is to ignore how much good can be achieved with the available resources. If scarcity is ignored, other patients who could benefit from other treatments will have to be left untreated. The moral claims of these patients will be ignored. They can just as well complain of unfairness. Their health care needs are neglected for the sake of benefits to others.

The argument that capacity to benefit from treatment is irrelevant has unpalatable implications. If it is accepted, a treatment that saves the lives of patients and enables them to live many years in good health will be no more important than a treatment that provides a few extra weeks at great cost. A treatment that drastically improves health-related quality of life will be no better than a treatment that leaves patients in constant pain and discomfort. If it does not matter how much benefit a treatment can provide, the health care system will expend a lot of resources on marginal benefits, leaving a lot of health needs unmet. In the absence of taking account of costs and benefits, health care can become a bottomless pit.

On reflection, it is difficult to accept that capacity to benefit from treatment is a morally irrelevant factor. Health-related quality of life is a morally relevant consideration. Other things being equal, the greater a person's capacity to benefit, the stronger her claim. It is not unfair to give priority to those who have a greater capacity to benefit. Neither is it unfair to take into account the number of those who have moral claims on treatment. If costs and benefits are ignored, many of these claims will not be satisfied. The health needs of many patients will not be met. This in itself is a form of unfairness, given that these needs could have been met.

It does not follow that capacity to benefit is all that matters. As we explained in the previous chapter, reducing inequality or giving priority to patients who are more severely ill are also relevant considerations. Being worse off than others might also make one's claim stronger. A person with a disability or chronic condition will often be worse off than others, and have stronger moral claims. And sometimes when patients, disabled or otherwise, cannot get the treatment they need, the right thing to do is to reduce scarcity by allocating more resources to the health care system.

Our argument is not that health care systems are always free of unfair discrimination against people with disabilities and chronic health conditions. Often, the opposite is the case. But the discrimination is not the consequence of using cost-effectiveness analysis. Rather, it is a consequence of directly excluding some patients due to their disability. In other words, the unfair discrimination is a consequence of unfair access. Perhaps the most conspicuous example is the practice, familiar from some health care systems, of health insurance providers denying coverage to people with preexisting conditions. In these systems, insurance providers are allowed not only to select the treatments they cover, but to select the patients they cover as well.

4.3 Fair innings

We have argued that the use of cost-effectiveness analysis does not lead to unfair discrimination against people with disabilities. We have also acknowledged, however, that selecting treatments sometimes unavoidably leads to the selection of patients. When treatment for the final stages of cancer is not deemed cost-effective, it is particular patients whose health needs get lower priority. Such cases raise questions of fairness. We have defended the view that it is not unfair to take health-related quality of life into account in resolving these questions.

Some critics of cost-effectiveness analysis believe there is another way that questions of fairness arise. According to their view, when Oregon ranked child health care services high and treatment for the final stages of AIDS low on its priority list, the problem was not that it unfairly discriminated in favor of children. Instead, the problem was that it did not go far enough. This is because, according to these critics, it is permissible to discriminate by age in the allocation of health care resources. While those who are at the end of a long life should not be abandoned, there should be limits on their share of society's resources, especially when they directly compete for those resources with younger people. Just as all players should get enough playtime in a friendly game, everyone should be given a chance to have a fair go at a long, complete life. Hence, if resources are scarce, it is justified to give priority to the young. This is the *fair innings argument*.

We will use simple examples to illustrate the argument. Consider first the following case. Suppose there are two life-saving treatments and two equally large groups of patients. Treatment A is needed by the first group, and Treatment B is needed by the second group. The only difference between the two groups is that the first consists of 20-year-old patients, and the second consists of 70-year-old patients. Everything else is equal: none of the patients is more deserving of the treatment, none of them has family responsibilities, none would survive without treatment, and so on. Moreover, the two treatments have the same costs, they do not have any side-effects, and both restore patients to full health.

Unfortunately, you can provide only one of the treatments. You can extend the lives of the patients in only one of the groups. That is, you have to choose between

(A) a treatment for the group of 20-year-old patients, all of whom will live for many years if they are treated;
(B) a treatment for the group of 70-year-old patients, all of whom will live for only a few more years if they are treated.

Most people agree that A should be chosen. If you cannot help all of the patients, it is more important to choose the treatment that saves the lives of younger patients. A cost-effectiveness analysis would make the same recommendation. Since Treatment A has a beneficial effect for a longer period, it provides more QALYs. Since everything else is equal, Treatment A has a better cost-effectiveness ratio. On this argument, discriminating in favor of the young is justified on benefit-maximizing grounds. Because of this, the argument is sometimes called *utilitarian ageism*.

Notice that in the example, cost-effectiveness analysis does not recommend the treatment for younger people because of health-related quality of life considerations. By assumption, all patients would be restored to full health. They would all be at the same health-related quality of life level. The treatment is favored because younger people have greater life expectancies than older people. What is at issue is the second component of the measurement of health benefits – the duration of treatment effect.

As it happens, defenders of the fair innings argument are often opponents of cost-effectiveness analysis. They do not believe that priority should be given to Treatment A because of benefit-maximizing considerations. They want to argue that giving priority to the young is a matter of *fairness*, rather than benefit maximization.

One reason defenders of the fair innings argument resist appealing to benefit maximization is that they typically hold that disability discrimination is unfair. They hold that health-related quality of life is an irrelevant consideration in health care resource allocation. But they also believe that treating people unequally because of their age is not unfair. Consequently, they must reject utilitarian ageism. If the fair innings argument was formulated in terms of maximizing benefits, its defenders would be open to the objection that they draw an arbitrary distinction between *quality* and *quantity* of life. If setting priorities by life expectancy is not unfair, why should setting priorities by health-related quality of life be unfair?

Another reason defenders of the fair innings argument resist appealing to benefit maximization is to avoid the *aggregation problem*. Benefit-maximizing views imply that in a choice between giving a large benefit to a few people (for instance, preventing their death) and giving small benefits to many people (for instance, curing their mild headaches), sometimes the small benefits to many people can outweigh the large benefits to the few. All it takes is a sufficient number of beneficiaries. But many people believe that *no* amount of small benefits to many people can outweigh large benefits to a few.

In the next chapter, we will discuss the aggregation problem in detail. For now, the important point is that defenders of the fair innings argument want to avoid the following sort of implication. Suppose the group of 70-year-old patients is sufficiently larger such that more QALYs would be produced if Treatment B was chosen. (Assume the costs remain the same.) Thus, on benefit-maximizing grounds, you would have to choose to save the 70-year-old patients, regardless of the fact that each 20-year-old patient would live for many more years than any 70-year-old patient.

But this is not what the fair innings argument is about. So its defenders want to resist this implication. Each 70-year-old has already had a long, complete life. If they are treated, no 20-year-old will have the chance to have a complete life. No number of the relatively small benefits that each of them would receive – a few extra years – should be able to outweigh the smaller number of large benefits that each 20-year-old would receive: many extra years.

Finally, there is an even more important reason to resist appealing to benefit maximization. The fair innings argument is not concerned with life expectancy. It is not concerned with the additional QALYs that different treatments may produce. Instead, it is concerned with age. Its defenders argue that it is the age of the beneficiary that makes a difference to the value of benefits.

To see this, consider the following example. Just as before, there are two equally large groups of patients. The first group consists of 20-year-old patients, and the second consists of 70-year-old patients. Everything else is equal. Once again, there are two treatments, each of which can extend the life of the patients in one of the groups. Just as before, you can provide only one of the treatments. You have to choose between

(C) a treatment for a group of 20-year-old patients, all of whom will live for ten more years if they are treated;
(D) a treatment for a group of 70-year-old patients, all of whom will live for ten more years if they are treated.

Since all patients would spend the remaining ten years of their lives in good health, there is no difference in expected benefit. Since everything else is equal, including the costs and the number of patients whose lives can be extended, the two treatments have the same cost-effectiveness ratio. Therefore, in terms of maximizing benefits, Treatment C and Treatment D are equally good. On these grounds, A is better than B, but C and D are equally good. This is the implication of utilitarian ageism.

But defenders of the fair innings argument believe not only that A should be chosen in the choice between A and B, but also that C should be chosen in the choice between C and D. Therefore, they have a separate view. On the basis of this view, they object to cost-effectiveness analysis because it is sensitive to life expectancy, but it is insensitive to age. They believe this gets things the wrong way around: health care resource allocation should be sensitive to age, but not to life expectancy.

The explanation for favoring Treatment C on the fair innings argument is this. There is a threshold that should be considered a *fair innings* – a length of life that is sufficient for a "complete" or "full" life. For example, the threshold might be at three score and ten, or 70 years. Having that lifespan is enough to carry out the major projects of life: finish school, build a career, start a family, and see one's children grow up and start families of their own. It is a reasonable amount of time for most life plans. A life that ends before has not had enough time for carrying out these plans and enjoying the pleasures distinctive of all ages. This is why it is a tragedy to die young.

On this argument, everyone should have a chance to reach their fair innings. But once they have, the strength of their claims on the rest of society sharply diminishes. Their health needs are given lower priority compared to the health needs of younger people. While no one would suggest that society should simply abandon them, it has been suggested that people over the fair innings threshold should be ineligible for expensive life-extending treatment. They should only be provided palliative care. The rest of their lives is a sort of "bonus time" without any obligation on the rest of us to maintain or extend.

An obvious question for this argument is why we should accept that there is a threshold of fair innings. If it is important that people are given an equal chance to complete their life plans, why is it not equally important that people are given an equal chance to complete more of their life plans even if they have no chance to fully complete them? If a person's age diminishes the strength of her claims after reaching the threshold, why should those who have lived less not have relatively stronger claims than those who have lived more, even if neither of them has yet reached the threshold?

To illustrate the problem, consider the following choice:

(E) a treatment for a group of 30-year-old patients, all of whom will live for ten more years if they are treated;

(F) a treatment for a group of 40-year-old patients, all of whom will live for ten more years if they are treated.

As before, everything else is equal.

A defender of utilitarian ageism holds that C, D, E and F are all equally good. A defender of the fair innings argument holds that C should be chosen in the choice between C and D. But when it comes to E and F, she does not hold that E should be chosen. This is not a choice in which either of the groups have already reached their fair innings. But it is not implausible to believe that E should be chosen: the 30-year-old patients do seem to have a complaint if they are not given priority compared to the 40-year-old patients. After all, they have had less of life than their older peers. Is that not unfair?

The idea of a fair innings threshold has been defended by appealing to an analogy. Suppose that two people are given the chance to run a mile, which most people can do in seven minutes. One of them is given four minutes, but the other is only given three. It is not true, however, that the former is given a "fairer" running time. It is no more possible to run a mile in four minutes than it is in three minutes. The unfairness to the second person is no greater than the unfairness to the first person.

The problem with this analogy is that it provides no new argument. It just restates the original claim that the fair innings should be a threshold. After all, the runners may value not only finishing the mile but covering as much ground as they can. While neither can hope to finish the whole mile in their time, it very much matters to them how much ground they can cover. Thus, if what is valuable is to give people a fair go at making the most of their lives, the 30-year-old patients will be disadvantaged. They have a stronger complaint than people who are given a longer time.

But perhaps there is another way to understand the analogy. Finishing the mile is not just valuable because you have run 1,609 meters. It is valuable because it is an achievement. But the value of that achievement does not come at any particular part of the distance. It comes from completing the whole distance. Thus, it is no more of an achievement to have reached 1,600 meters than it is to have reached 1,599 meters.

Similarly, much that is valuable in life does not accumulate like steps taken toward the mile. The full value that bringing up children, or writing a book, or undertaking some important project adds to a life only appears at their completion. If these plans and projects cannot be completed, you lose more than the value they would bring during the time until their completion. You lose the value of the whole, completed project. This is why a *complete* life is valuable. Death at the end of a complete life is regrettable, but not a tragedy. Death before a life can be complete is a tragedy.

But this defense of the fair innings threshold leads to another difficulty. Consider another variation of the sort of cases we have been using. Suppose that the fair innings threshold is 70, and this time you have to choose between

(G) a treatment for a group of 30-year-old patients, all of whom will live for ten more years if they are treated;
(H) a treatment for a group of 60-year-old patients, all of whom will live for ten more years if they are treated.

The defender of the fair innings argument is committed to the idea that the full value of having a complete life cannot come before the threshold is reached. In this example, the 60-year-old patients can turn the argument on its head. They can argue that even though neither they nor the 30-year-old patients have reached the threshold, their treatment should be given priority. After all, the 60-year-old patients, and only them, could just achieve a complete life with all its value. In contrast, the 30-year-old patients have no chance for a complete life at all. The 60-year-old patients can argue that if death before the fair innings threshold is a tragedy, then their treatment should be chosen, since that way there will be only half as many tragedies. That is, even though the defenders of the threshold should officially hold that the fair innings argument does not require giving priority to either G or H, their view arguably implies that H should be chosen.

We do not think many people would accept this argument. For one thing, the badness of tragedies should not be counted this way. But even setting this aside, the difficulty remains. The defender of the fair innings argument holds that neither G nor H requires priority on her view. We have argued that her view might actually imply that H should be given priority. Even if we are wrong about that, many people would argue that in the choice between G and H, Treatment G should be chosen. Either way, the fair innings argument has implausible implications.

Longevity is valuable, but it is not a matter of thresholds. Life is not like a race, where achievement is the overriding aim. Human plans and projects are open-ended, and we value them for their own sake. We hope to be able to complete them, but we also value undertaking them.

The problem with utilitarian ageism is that it is insensitive to age. It is sensitive only to life expectancy. The fair innings argument is sensitive to age, but below the threshold it is insensitive to life expectancy. But perhaps both age and life expectancy matter. We should look for a way to take both into account.

In order to do that, we do not have to abandon cost-effectiveness analysis. We can apply the idea of equity weights that we introduced in the previous chapter. Figure 4.1 reproduces the illustration that we used to explain it, applied to the choice between C and D.

In this figure, the horizontal axis represents life years. The further a point is from the origin, the more years a person has already lived. Thus, the interval between 20 and 30 on the horizontal axis represents the ten years that 20-year-old patients can survive for if they receive treatment C; the interval between 70 and 80 represents the ten years that 70-year-old patients can survive for if they receive Treatment D. The vertical axis represents the moral value of the additional years that the patients would have.

The left-hand side of the figure represents utilitarian ageism. The moral value of the additional years that would be gained by the 20-year-old patients, v(C), equals the moral value of the additional years that would be gained by the 70-year-old patients, v(D). These benefits are equally valuable since they consist of the same number of additional years. If the

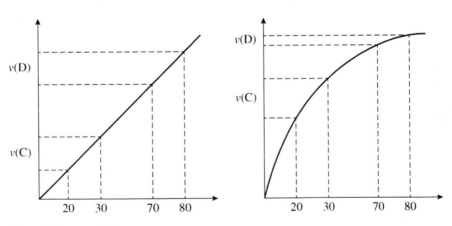

Figure 4.1 Age-weighting.

younger patients could survive for many more years, as in the choice between A and B, the interval representing their additional years would be extended beyond 30, further away from the origin. Since there would be more additional years for younger patients, their treatment would be better.

The right-hand side of the figure illustrates the application of equity weights to life years – or *age weights*, as they are often called. On the view this represents, additional life years have extra value, but their value diminishes at higher ages. This view gives priority to younger people. So, if the graph represents the choice between a treatment like C that enables 20-year-old patients to live for ten more years, and a treatment like D that enables 70-year-old patients to live for ten more years, then the value of the first treatment is greater.

Just like utilitarian ageism, this view holds that A is better than B; just like the fair innings argument, it holds that in the choice between A and B, A should be chosen. But contrary to utilitarian ageism, it also holds that C is better than D, E is better than F, and G is better than H. And contrary to the fair innings argument, this view does not hold that neither E nor F, and neither G nor H, should get higher priority. Arguably, this view accords better with people's moral intuitions about the significance of age.

To the best of our knowledge, this sort of age-weighting has never been used in practice. A somewhat similar form of age-weighting was, however, used in the Global Burden of Disease studies. But its rationale was different, and it became very controversial.

4.4 Age-weighting and the burden of disease

As we explained in Chapter 2, DALYs are a measure of the burden of premature mortality and morbidity from disease and injury. They can be used as a summary measure of population health and as an outcome measure in cost-effectiveness analysis. A unique feature of the DALYs used in the early Global Burden of Disease studies was that they had different weights at different ages.

A DALY is a combination of years of life lost due to premature mortality and years of life lived with disability. Disabilities represent the effect of different conditions on people's ability to carry out common or normal activities. The DALYs associated with a particular disease are the sum of the years of life lost due to premature mortality caused by that disease, and the years of life lived with the disability caused by that disease, adjusted for its disability weight.

DALYs are a *gap measure* – they represent the shortfall from perfect or ideal health. The closer the disability weights are to 0, the smaller the shortfall in health. The younger a person dies because of a disease, the greater the number of years of life lost due to premature mortality. Years of life lost represent the gap between actual mortality and ideal life expectancy. Thus, the gap associated with premature mortality is determined by the ideal, maximum age beyond which death is not considered premature.

Currently, the ideal life expectancy at birth is set at 86 years. This is the number of years of life lost in the case of infant mortality. But life expectancy changes as people age: at higher ages, life expectancies are relatively higher for people who have survived to that age. Thus, at age 50, the life expectancy on the basis of which years of life lost are calculated is just over 37 years.

For a long time, DALYs were *age-weighted*: they were given different weights according to age at the onset of disease – or, in the case of premature mortality, according to the age at which a person is killed by disease. So it would not be accurate to say that the burden of premature mortality at 50 is 37 years of life lost. The actual burden of this death would have been smaller, because DALYs over 50 had smaller weights.

In fact, the age-weighting function in the Global Burden of Disease studies had a particular form. It gave the greatest weight to DALYs between the ages of 20 and 30, peaking around age 25. After 30, the weights steadily diminished. Thus, the relative value of a year around 20 was approximately one and a half of the relative value of a year around 60. But unlike the sort of weighting that the fair innings argument would imply, DALYs were given smaller weights under ages 20. A DALY had a smaller weight at ages 5, 10, or 15 than at 20 or 30. The age-weighting function was "hump-shaped": it began at a low value at birth, increased until 25–30, and then steadily decreased as age increased.

Plainly, these weights cannot be justified on the basis of the fair innings argument, since the weights were smaller for children who have not reached their fair innings.

Age-weighting in the Global Burden of Disease studies became very controversial. Critics attacked it both because of the shape of the age-weighting function and because of the justification that the developers of DALYs offered for taking age into account.

So why should the health of people in young adulthood be more important than their health in childhood, or middle and old ages? Why should a disease or injury be *less bad* if it affects a child or an old person?

One justification may be that people's economic productivity varies at different ages. Children and adolescents normally do not yet work; older people are often retired and rely on their savings, pensions, or adult children for support. People are most productive in their adulthood. Therefore, it is not unjustified to consider their health at this age more important, since death or disability at this stage of life has a greater social and economic impact. This is known as the *human capital argument*.

The developers of the DALY did not accept the human capital argument, but not because they thought it was unfair to consider the impact of ill-health on productivity at different ages. On the contrary, they argued that the problem with the human capital argument is that it is too narrow: it ignores the non-economic benefits that young adults create. In particular, it ignores the fact that young adults often take care of their children and elderly parents. Focusing on economic benefits only does not capture the full range of their contributions to the well-being of others.

In their interpretation, age-weighting captures *welfare interdependence* – the many ways the well-being of children and the elderly depends on young adults. They argued that the value of the health of a 30-year-old person should be greater than the value of the health of a 60-year-old person, because the 30-year-old contributes more to the well-being of others. Thus, a disease or injury when you are 30 is worse than the same disease or injury when you are 60. With age-weighting, a DALY for someone at this age has greater value – that is, it is a greater burden.

The argument from welfare interdependence suffers from several problems. For one thing, it is not true in all societies that young adults take the lion's share of ensuring the well-being of others. Older generations often provide substantial support to their children and grandchildren. In some societies, people remain active well into their old age. Age-weighting DALYs may be a form of cultural bias.

An even greater problem is that DALYs are not supposed to capture the way a person contributes to the well-being of others. DALYs represent the burden of mortality and morbidity. Contributions to economic and other sources of welfare have no place in such a measure. The DALY is a measure of health-related quality of life, and not overall well-being. It should capture the burden of a disease or injury *for the patient*, and not how the disease or injury affects others.

Some critics argue that even if age-weighting is justifiable, the particular form of the age-weighting function selected by the developers of the DALY leads to unfair discrimination against children and adolescents. Suppose, for instance, that an old person suffers from the same disease for the same amount of time as a young adult. Because of age-weighting, her years of life lived with disability have a smaller weight, and treating her has lower priority, since it leads to a smaller DALY reduction. One could argue, however, that older people cannot complain if they are given lower priority, since their DALYs were given a greater weight when they were young adults. They have already benefited from age-weighting – or at least, they would have benefited from it if they had the disability as young adults.

But the age-weighting function gives a smaller weight to the DALYs of children and adolescents as well. If a child suffers from the same condition for the same amount of time as a young adult, her years of life lived with disability also have a smaller weight. Treating her has lower priority, since it leads to a smaller DALY reduction. But in this case, it is not true that she has benefited from age-weighting: her DALYs have not been given (or would have been given) a greater weight at any previous time. If she dies as a result of her disease, she cannot even be potentially compensated. Arguably, this is a case of unfair discrimination.

Age-weighting became one of the most controversial issues in the measurement of the burden of disease. The experts working in the Disease Control Priorities Project (described in the previous chapter) do not use age weights at all. Because of the many arguments marshaled against it, the Global Burden of Disease project also abandoned age-weighting from its 2010 update. This decision has a major effect on the way the harms of mortality and morbidity are calculated worldwide. It is also one of the few examples when the arguments of philosophers have made a big difference in the real world.

4.5 Further moral considerations

In the last two chapters, we have focused on cost-effectiveness analysis. We explained how it works. We introduced some real-life examples of its use. We have defended it from several objections. We explored ways to extend it in order to take other moral considerations into account.

We have been assuming that the maximization of health benefits is an important objective of health care resource allocation. Scarce resources should be used for interventions and health care services that provide the best value for money. But we have also made it clear that this is not the only objective. Other moral considerations are also important, and it cannot be expected that cost-effectiveness analysis can take care of them all.

This is because cost-effectiveness analysis is not merely a technical tool. It implicitly incorporates value judgments and ethical ideas. When it uses QALYs or DALYs as its measure of health benefit, they bring with them the consequences of all the value judgments and simplifying assumptions that went into their construction. Moreover, cost-effectiveness calculations rely on value judgments of their own. Most importantly, standard cost-effectiveness analysis assumes that all health benefits have the same value, regardless of their distribution.

This assumption is a matter of moral judgment. You may reasonably disagree with it. For instance, you might believe that the health needs of those who have a more severe illness are especially urgent. Or you might believe that health care resources should be allocated in a way that reduces inequalities in health. We have argued that it is possible to modify cost-effectiveness analysis to take into account these moral judgments. Equity weights can do this. In practice, equity weighting could be used to give more weight to interventions and health care services that primarily benefit those who are worse off, or those that reduce health inequalities.

Standard cost-effectiveness analysis also assumes that all health benefits have the same value, regardless of the age of the beneficiary. This is also a moral judgment, and once again you might reasonably disagree with it. You may be impressed by some form of the fair innings argument, or the idea that differences in the way people contribute to the well-being of others at different ages should be taken into account.

Although we have argued against a fair innings threshold and the way DALYs used to be given different weights at different ages, we have also shown that it is possible to modify cost-effectiveness analysis to take into account the moral significance of age. You can do this by introducing age weights. In practice, age-weighting could be used to give more weight to interventions and health care services that primarily benefit younger people.

The disability discrimination objection seems more serious. It claims that the use of cost-effectiveness analysis leads to unfair discrimination against patients with disabilities and long-term chronic conditions. But in our view, this objection is mistaken. Cost-effectiveness analysis ranks interventions, not patients or patient groups. It does not inherently discriminate against anyone. True, some patients may have to forgo beneficial treatments – but that is a consequence of scarcity or lack of access, not the use of cost-effectiveness analysis. If you refused to take into account benefits and costs, there would be even more patients who have to forgo beneficial treatments.

Nevertheless, we have acknowledged that discrimination against some patient groups may result *indirectly* – as an unintended practical consequence of the way the costs and benefits work out. For instance, treating some diseases or disabilities may be less cost-effective only because they are rare, so that there has not been enough research or experience in their treatment. There might also be some patient groups who are disproportionately burdened by particular diseases or disabilities. Some groups might be susceptible to conditions that do not affect others at all.

The best way to make sure that these health needs are not ignored is to consider them *in addition to* cost-effectiveness considerations. Thus, cost-effectiveness analysis should not be rejected. But it might need to be supplemented. Once you have ranked all the interventions, you should look at the outcomes of allocating health care resources according to your priority list. Are there any outcomes for particular groups that seem unfair? If there are, you ought to modify your priorities to avoid them.

Philosophers and health policy experts have offered a number of additional ethical considerations for supplementing cost-effectiveness analysis. We will discuss some of the most salient here. Other considerations might arise in particular circumstances.

Here is one consideration. Standard cost-effectiveness analysis is *forward-looking*: it takes into account the prospective health benefits from particular interventions and the costs of introducing the interventions. It does not consider the past health of the patients who would benefit from the interventions. But you might believe that an intervention may be particularly important because the patients who need it have suffered significant health loss in the past. For instance, they may have suffered from a permanent disability or long-term chronic condition. Compared to other interventions that have comparable benefits and costs, an intervention that targets patients with significant past health loss should have higher priority.

You may justify the relevance of past health by appealing to the idea that people should have a fair chance to have a long, healthy life. Those who have suffered in the past from poor health should have stronger claims on health care resources, because their poor health has limited their opportunities for flourishing. If you are in a position to improve their health, you should not ignore this fact.

Other considerations relate to the characteristics of particular patient groups. We already mentioned one consideration at the beginning of Chapter 1. There we asked you to consider vaccination programs for children. We can assume that the vaccination programs considered in the example were highly cost-effective: they protected children from a fatal disease. But while some of the children were easy to reach, others lived in remote areas. This would not make a difference to the cost-effectiveness calculations of the vaccinations (since standard cost-effectiveness analysis does not separate patients into different groups), but it might make a difference in access and delivery. In particular, you might believe that children in remote areas should also be given a fair chance of getting the vaccinations. To ensure that there are enough funds for this, you might want to give a high priority to the vaccination programs.

A particularly important consideration is gender equality. Although maternal and child health care services tend to have very favorable cost-effectiveness ratios, reproductive health is more than a health issue. Reproductive health services influence equality of opportunity, gender inequality, and women's rights. They are also divisive political issues in many countries. Because of their broader social and political implications for social justice, their provision is not merely a matter of costs and benefits.

Moreover, disability, disease, and injury can have catastrophic consequences for patients and their families. They can push middle-class families into poverty, and poor families into deeper poverty. Cost-effectiveness analysis does not evaluate the financial consequences of interventions for patients. That is a separate issue about sharing the costs between individuals and their communities. It is often argued that higher priority should be given to interventions and health care services that protect patients and households from catastrophic medical expenses. Others, however, argue that the best way to address this issue is not by tinkering with cost-effectiveness calculations, but by implementing fair financing mechanisms in health care and by increasing the health care budget.

This example also reveals the limitations of our discussion so far. Health care resource allocation is extremely complex, and cost-effectiveness calculations are only a small part of it. There are many other moral questions that arise in health care. Some of these will be introduced in Chapter 6. But before we get there, we have to address a more general ethical problem.

At the beginning of this section, we said that we had been assuming that one of the most important objectives of the allocation of health care resources is the maximization of health benefits. Cost-effectiveness analysis is a tool that can be used to rank interventions in a way that best achieves this objective. But we have not defended the moral principle of benefit maximization. We have, indeed, just assumed it.

In particular, the principle of benefit maximization assumes that benefits for different people can be added together. Applied to health, the principle assumes that QALYs for different people, for instance, can be added. This is a very controversial claim in ethics. We need to defend it. That is the task for Chapter 5.

Chapter summary

This chapter discussed two criticisms of the use of cost-effectiveness analysis for the allocation of health care resources. According to the first objection, the use of cost-effectiveness calculations leads to unfair discrimination against people with disabilities. We showed that this objection is either based on misunderstanding the way cost-effectiveness analysis works or it does not provide a decisive objection to it. Another criticism focuses on discrimination by age. Proponents of the fair innings argument contend that those who have reached old age should have weaker claims on health care resources. We argued against the traditional formulation of this argument, but we also showed how age-weighting can be introduced to make it less objectionable. At the same time, we rejected the reasons for age-weighting DALYs.

This chapter concludes our extended discussion of cost-effectiveness analysis. It is important to keep in mind that we did not claim that cost-effectiveness analysis is the only moral principle for the allocation of health care resources. We concluded by presenting some moral considerations that may also have a role in the ethical rationing of health care.

Discussion questions

1. One rationing principle is "first come, first served": resources are allocated in the order that health needs arise. Thus, for instance, first come, first served could be used to organize patients into a waiting list: those who have been on the list longer have higher priority. Is this an acceptable ethical principle? Does it lead to unfair treatment of some patients?
2. Many people believe that it is less of a tragedy if a very small child dies than if a teenager dies. These people, in fact, appear to believe that the life of a teenager is more valuable than the life of a very small child. What reasons could be given for this view? Is it acceptable from a moral point of view?
3. Suppose there are two patients with the same health condition. They are the same age, they are equally severely ill, and their health outcomes would be the same if they are treated or left untreated. The only difference between the two patients is that one has had this health condition for a longer time than the other. If you can only treat one of them, should this be a relevant consideration?
4. In most societies, life expectancies differ between men and women: women can expect to live longer – by several years, in some cases. Part of this difference is apparently biologically determined, and part of it is due to the fact that men are more likely to take risks with their health. Does this difference raise any ethical concern? Should social policies aim to narrow the gap in life expectancies between men and women?
5. One of the criticisms of market-based health insurance is that health insurance providers can refuse to cover people with preexisting conditions. Many people argue that this is a form of unfair discrimination against people with pre-existing health problems. Do you agree? What makes this practice unfair?

Further readings

An excellent overview of the disability discrimination objection is Brock (2009); see also Brock (2004). Perhaps the most forceful formulation of the disability discrimination objection is to be found in Harris (1987); for a reply to Harris, see Singer *et al.* (1995) as well as McKie *et al.* (1998). For other contributions to the debate, see Bognar (2010, 2011). The formulation in the text of the original fair innings argument is based on Harris (1985). See also Broome (1988), Kappel and Sandøe (1992), and McKerlie (2013). Bognar (2008*a*) discusses both the fair innings argument and the age-weighting of DALYs.

Notes

1 Phillips (2006, p. 47, emphasis in original).

2 Quoted in "U.S. Backs Oregon's Health Plan for Covering All Poor People," *The New York Times*, March 20, 1993.

3 Quoted in Brock (2009, p. 29); the original is a press release issued by Louis Sullivan of the Health and Human Services Press Office on August 3, 1992.

5   The aggregation of health benefits

5.1 The aggregation problem

Cost-effectiveness analysis rests on the idea that health care resources should be allocated in a way that provides the best value for money – in the way that maximizes the health benefits in the population. In practice, cost-effectiveness analysis is used to select those interventions and health care services that provide the most benefit for the lowest costs. You can use it, like NICE does, to evaluate new interventions, technologies, diagnostic procedures, pharmaceuticals, and so on. In the Oregon Medi-caid reform, a list of 709 treatments was drawn up and the top 587 were selected. These were to be provided to all eligible residents of the state. By broadening access and limiting the available treatments and services, the aim of the Oregon Health Plan was to maximize health benefits in the population of eligible residents.

The Oregon Health Plan received a lot of criticism. In the previous chapter, we discussed some of the objections. But there was another objection that we have not yet addressed.

To many critics, Oregon's priority list of treatment-condition pairs was itself questionable. They argued that it was unclear how some parts of the rankings could be justified from an ethical point of view. One example that received a lot of attention compared dental caps for pulp exposure and surgical treatment for appendicitis. On Oregon's list, the former was ranked higher than the latter. But ranking tooth capping higher than appendectomy seemed counterintuitive to many people, because appendectomy is far more urgent and important than tooth capping. After all, appendectomy is an effective, low-risk treatment for a potentially life-threatening condition, while tooth capping addresses a relatively minor ailment. There is something wrong, the critics argued, with the ranking of these two treatments.

Why were the two conditions ranked this way? The answer is that the ranking was a consequence of cost-effectiveness analysis. Recall that cost-effectiveness analysis takes into account the costs of an intervention and its health benefits. The benefits are expressed in terms of some combined measure of the impact of the intervention on health-related quality of life and the duration of the impact. The costs are divided by the benefits; the lower the ratio, the more cost-effective the intervention is.

Here is how the treatments were evaluated on the list. In Oregon's calculation, the expected health benefit of tooth capping was 0.08 on a scale between 0 and 1 (the closer the value is to 1, the greater the benefit). The expected duration of the benefit was four years. Thus, the expected health benefit of a tooth capping was 0.32 QALYs. Its cost was $38.10.

The expected health benefit of an appendectomy, in contrast, was 0.97 on the 0–1 scale. That is not surprising, since appendectomies save lives. The expected duration of the benefit was 48 years. Thus, an appendectomy's expected health benefit was 46.56 QALYs. But one appendectomy costs $5,744.

An appendectomy is a much greater benefit than a tooth capping – 46.56 versus 0.32 QALYs. But it is also much more expensive – $5,744 versus $38.10. Their cost-effectiveness depends on the ratio of their costs and benefits. For tooth capping, the ratio is slightly over 119; for an appendectomy, the ratio is over 123. Since the lower the ratio, the better, tooth cappings are more cost-effective than appendectomies. In Oregon's priority list, tooth capping was item 371, and appendectomy was item 377.

Before we go on, it is important to see what the objection is. After all, Oregon planned to cover all items between 1 and 587 on its priority list. No patient with appendicitis would have been denied treatment. The fact that this was the best example the critics could find is evidence that there was no similar discrepancy in the items below 587.

Nevertheless, the critics did have a point. Suppose a similar priority list is implemented in a resource-poor setting. Suppose also that health benefits are maximized by giving priority to meeting the needs that correspond to higher-ranked items on the list. As it happens, item 371 (tooth capping), is provided to every patient who needs it. But then, before reaching item 377, you run out of funds. This might be because many people need tooth capping. As a consequence, the smaller number of patients with appendicitis cannot be treated. They die. Let us call this the appendectomy/tooth capping case.

This is obviously a simplified example. It is important to emphasize that in real life, health care resources are allocated in a much more complex way. You do not simply go down the list, selecting which patients to treat first. You do not withhold appendectomies until everyone is given dental caps. That would be absurd. In this respect, the example that critics latched onto is a bit misleading.

Still, the appendectomy/tooth capping case illustrates an important moral objection. In our imagined story, appendectomies are not provided because too many people need tooth capping. Since tooth capping has a better cost-effectiveness ratio, it has higher priority. From the perspective of maximizing health benefits, ranking tooth capping higher than appendectomies is justified.

This seemingly counterintuitive argument reflects the following ethical thesis: benefits to different people can be added up and compared across different groups, and it is morally acceptable to make ethical judgments on the basis of such interpersonally aggregated benefits. Let us call this the *aggregation thesis*. A direct implication of it is that very small benefits to a great number of people can outweigh far more significant benefits to a few people.

Is the aggregation thesis justifiable? Some philosophers argue that it is. You are allowed to compare the aggregated benefits of different groups in order to identify the best pattern of resource allocation. Other philosophers argue that the aggregation thesis is not justifiable, and you are not allowed to compare the total benefits of different groups. The debate concerning the implications of the aggregation thesis is known as the *aggregation problem*.

We have argued that the use of cost-effectiveness analysis rests on the principle of benefit maximization. As a consequence, it presupposes the aggregation thesis. Thus, it accepts that if the costs are equal, a greater sum of small QALY improvements for many people (like tooth cappings) is better than a smaller sum of great QALY improvements for a few people (like appendectomies). It accepts that a greater sum of smaller DALY reductions for many people is better than a smaller sum of great DALY reductions for a few. In the practice of estimating overall health benefits, the aggregation thesis is taken for granted.

Utilitarianism also supports the aggregation thesis. Equity-weighted QALYs do as well, since they allow the aggregation of equity-weighted QALYs. Age-weighted QALYs or DALYs are the same.

Here is a typical objection to the aggregation thesis. If you accept the aggregation thesis, then, allegedly, you must also accept the judgment that it is right to carve up a healthy person and transplant his organs to five needy patients. This is because the aggregation thesis allows you to judge that the goodness of saving the lives of five patients outweighs the badness of one person's death. But this is utterly counterintuitive and obviously morally wrong. Critics, thus, argue that you must reject the aggregation thesis in order to avoid this sort of implausible moral judgment. In the appendectomy/tooth capping case, critics contend that the health benefits of tooth capping for many people are not permitted to outweigh the health benefits of appendectomy for a few people, regardless of the numbers of people who require tooth capping. Thus, they conclude that it is wrong to rank tooth capping above appendectomy. Appendectomy should be ranked above tooth capping.

What alternative moral principle can critics of the aggregation thesis support? After all, they too have to be able to give you guidance for resource allocation choices. Surely, their alternative principle must be non-aggregative and hence insensitive to the numbers of people who are affected by your choice. Here is one: the *principle of pairwise comparison*. The basic idea is to find the outcome that is the least unacceptable from individual standpoints. When there is a conflict of interests amongst different persons, no outcome can be completely acceptable to everyone. What you have to do is to focus on a pair of people who are affected by the choice, and compare one person's possible loss to the other person's possible loss in order to identify the outcome that minimizes the loss to each person. By continuing this pairwise (that is, one-to-one) comparison for every pair of affected people, you can identify the outcome that minimizes the greatest loss. The outcome that minimizes the maximum loss, according to the principle of pairwise comparison, is the least unacceptable from each person's separate point of view.

For example, suppose you are faced with a choice between saving the life of one person by appendectomy (let us call this person David) and reducing pain for 1,000 people by tooth capping. Suppose resources are insufficient to do both. You have to choose between providing the tooth cappings and providing the appendectomy. So, there is conflict of interests between David and 1,000 people with toothache.

Proponents of the aggregation thesis claim that it can be right to offer the tooth capping to the 1,000 people. The principle of pairwise comparison, in contrast, implies that it is morally right to save the life of David. Compare the possible loss to David and the possible loss to each one of those who require tooth capping. If you choose to provide the tooth cappings, David will die. This is, obviously, a huge loss to David. If you choose to save David's life, each one of 1,000 people will suffer from toothache. But this is a comparatively small loss. Choosing to save David's life minimizes the maximum loss. Thus, according to the principle of pairwise comparison, choosing to save David's life is the least unacceptable alternative, considered from each person's point of view separately. The principle contends that it is right to choose to save David's life, no matter how many people need the tooth capping. As the number of people with toothache does not affect your judgment, the principle does not include the aggregation thesis. Therefore, it can be seen as a clear alternative to benefit maximization.

Initially, it appeared counterintuitive to give greater priority to tooth capping than to appendectomy. Many people's initial intuition is that appendectomy must be ranked above tooth capping. If this intuition is correct, the principle of pairwise comparison is more appealing than benefit maximization or utilitarian principles.

However, on reflection, our initial intuition may not be strong enough. The principle of pairwise comparison says that you should give priority to appendectomy over tooth capping, no matter how many people require the latter treatment. Some people are not so sure about this. Of course, if only ten people require tooth capping, you may well choose to save the life of one person. However, if 100,000 people suffer from toothaches, your initial intuition might become less firm. You might start preferring tooth capping to appendectomy. Or you might change your judgment only when the number increases to a million. The point is that if you think that there must be a sufficiently large number of people whose aggregated health benefits can outweigh the loss of one life, then you cannot accept the principle of pairwise comparison.

To be sure, you might not be able to identify the exact number of people with toothache that can outweigh the loss of one life. It may be 11 or 146 or one billion. However, the aggregation problem arises because of these conflicting intuitions about the comparison of benefits with different sizes.

5.2 The number problem

The cost of rejecting the aggregation thesis turns out to be serious. Here is a difficult problem for the critics of the aggregation thesis, which has become known as the *number problem*.

Suppose there are six fatally ill patients, who require a drug urgently. They are located in two places. There is one patient at one location and five patients at the other. You have a drug that can extend the life of each patient by 20 years. The health benefit for each patient is thus the same. You have enough drugs for all. Unfortunately, however, it is not possible to reach both of the locations because of lack of time. Thus, you are faced with the choice between extending the lives of five patients by 20 years or the life of one patient by 20 years. For the sake of simplicity, suppose that there are no morally relevant differences between these patients. They are all the same age. They would all be completely healthy in their remaining 20 years. None of them is a criminal, a Nobel prize winner, your child, friend, or parent.

Let us call this example the *rescue case*. Its difference from the appendectomy/tooth capping case is that in the rescue case, what should determine your course of action is the number of affected patients and nothing else. Intuitively, many people think that the drug should be given to the five patients. Even if the one person dies, you are not responsible for his death. You do not kill him. You just let him die. Of course, the death of the one person is a bad thing to happen. But the added gains from prolonging five lives can easily compensate for the loss of one life, and a large net gain can be obtained by extending the lives of five people. Because of this, many people think that it is right to choose the greater number of people.

But this reasoning presupposes the aggregation thesis. In this case, the intuition of many people reflects the aggregation thesis. For these people, the numbers really do matter.

What do critics of the aggregation thesis say about this example? Many critics agree with the popular intuition: it is morally right to give the drug to the five patients. But what they actually say seems inconsistent with what they have to say. Critics of the aggregation thesis are supposed to happily ignore the number of affected people. In the rescue case, the only difference between the two sides is the number of patients, which they are supposed to ignore. From what they have claimed, they have to be indifferent between extending the lives of five patients and extending the life of one patient, because the possible loss is the same for every patient. If they are indifferent, they should probably flip a fair coin to decide whom to treat, because the coin toss gives an equal chance of being saved to every patient. But this is counterintuitive.

To confirm this argument, consider what the principle of pairwise comparison would claim in the rescue case. This principle is number-insensitive. The gain and loss for each of the six patients are the same. The rescue case stipulates that there are no relevant differences between the six patients. From each individual standpoint, the size of loss is the same, no matter who receives the drug. Therefore, extending the life of one patient is just as acceptable (or unacceptable) as extending the lives of five patients. According to the principle of pairwise comparison, you should be indifferent between extending the lives of the five and extending the life of the one patient.

Now the critics of the aggregation thesis have a serious problem. They intuitively think that it is right to save the greater number of people, but their intuition is inconsistent with their criticism of the aggregation thesis. This is the number problem.

Can the problem be solved without appealing to the aggregation thesis? Here is one argument worth examining. Consider a situation where your choice is between extending the life of David for 20 years and extending the life of Emily for 20 years. As before, all other things are equal. In this case, it would be perfectly acceptable to flip a fair coin to decide whose life you extend. Now imagine that four different persons were added to the side of Emily. The choice becomes one between preventing five deaths and preventing David's death. If you are still indifferent, you will be open to the charge that you are ignoring the four additional persons. Just like David and Emily, they need your help. They have a moral claim for your assistance. Ignoring their moral claims is unacceptable from the perspective of each one of the four additional persons. Thus, by choosing to extend the lives of the five people, you recognize the claims of the four additional people and give a positive moral weight to their lives. Given that the size of the benefit is the same for all, saving the greater number is a principle that nobody could reasonably reject from her own individual standpoint. This is called the *tie-breaking argument* in the number problem.

The tie-breaking argument sounds pretty good. It does not add up the benefits of different people. Thus, it is non-aggregative. It appeals only to the moral claim of each person. However, two objections can be raised. First, you can argue that the tie-breaking argument is in fact aggregative – or at least it includes a comparison of the benefits of groups of people. If the choice were between David's life and Emily's life, everyone would agree that it is right to flip a fair coin. But on the argument under consideration, the claims of four additional people tip the balance in favor of the five people when presented in combination with Emily's claim. That is, the argument does compare a group of five with David. If this interpretation is correct, the tie-breaking argument is based on a sort of group aggregation. Therefore, it implicitly appeals to aggregation.

Second, for the sake of argument, let us accept the reasoning behind the tie-breaking argument. Suppose that you are faced with a choice between prolonging the lives of five people and prolonging the lives of two people. Now, according to the argument under consideration, if your choice was between the lives of five people and the life of one person, then you should extend the lives of the five people. But one additional person is added now to the side of the one person. If you still should choose the five lives, the presence of one additional person does not make any difference to what you should do. Therefore, the additional person's moral claim is ignored. For this additional person, saving the greater number is not acceptable. Her moral claim is not recognized at all. Therefore, the argument does not establish the conclusion that you should always choose the greater number. In this second objection, we have used the process of reasoning in the tie-breaking argument in order to refute its conclusion. The tie-breaking argument, after all, does not solve the problem.

Some people might claim that this second objection can be avoided if the tie-breaking is understood as *neutralizing*. In the choice between prolonging the lives of five people and prolonging the lives of two people, the claims of two people on either side are seen as "neutralizing" one another, and hence the claims of the three remaining persons tip the balance in favor of the five people. If the tie-breaking argument is interpreted this way, then it will always recommend choosing the greater number of people.

But this interpretation is unsatisfactory. The argument is still based on a sort of aggregation because it compares the group of five with the group of two directly.

We have now reached the stage where the fundamental issue with regards to the aggregation problem and the number problem can be understood. Intuitively, many people find it implausible to rank tooth capping above appendectomy. If their intuition is correct, the aggregation thesis, which underlies this ostensibly implausible ranking, should be rejected. But if the aggregation thesis is rejected, we run into a different counterintuitive implication: we should be indifferent between preventing many deaths and preventing fewer deaths. Should we revise our initial intuition in the appendectomy/tooth capping case and accept the aggregation thesis? Or should we continue to reject the aggregation thesis and give up our intuition for benefiting the greater number? It is hard to make up our mind.

At this stage, some people might be tempted to offer another solution. The aggregation problem, they argue, involves a comparison between health improvements and the prevention of death. The number problem, in contrast, involves only comparisons of preventing death. You should accept the aggregation thesis in the number problem when only lives are at stake. You should also accept the thesis when only health improvements are at stake. It is permissible to count the number of people whose life you can save, and it is also permissible to add up health benefits. But it is not permissible to compare health improvements and the prevention of death. You should reject the aggregation thesis in the aggregation problem.

Thus, there is no real inconsistency. Our argument rests on the fact that inconsistency in ethics must be avoided, since, as we explained in Chapter 1, inconsistent moral judgments are arbitrary. But, one could argue, there is no inconsistency if we give *absolute* priority to the prevention of death compared to health improvements. Appendectomies are one thing, and tooth cappings are another. They should not be on the same list. Or, if they must, the top items on a priority list should be reserved for interventions that prevent death.

This solution looks neat. It seems to avoid the inconsistency. As a matter of fact, something like this happened to Oregon's priority list after its first version was rejected by the federal government. Interventions were arranged into different categories according to their perceived importance. The top category included treatments for acute life-threatening conditions where the treatment prevented imminent death with full recovery or return to the previous health state. Appendectomy was placed in this category. As we mentioned in Chapter 3, cost-effectiveness considerations were largely abandoned from the revised priority list, since costs and resulting quality of life were not considered. Nonetheless, critics argued that the revised list is more acceptable. The proposal of separating life-saving interventions and health-improving interventions seems to provide its moral justification. It seems to accord better with most people's intuitions.

Yet the proposal does not work. It is easy to see why. Suppose you give absolute priority to interventions that prevent death. You do not allow any comparison of the benefits of mere health improvements and the benefits of saving lives. Chances are, you are never going to get to providing any interventions that merely improve health. If life has absolute value, you should spend all your resources on preventing death. You will do everything in your power to keep people alive, regardless of their quality of life. Treatments that postpone death but result in terrible pain and suffering will be more valuable than treatments that prevent or manage disability or chronic illness. Since postponing death can be very expensive – it requires expensive medicine, advanced technology, complex surgeries – you will soon exhaust your health care budget. You will have nothing left for maternal and child health care, pain management, or the myriad other forms of health care that can make lives better.

No one really believes that preventing death should have absolute priority, regardless of quality of life and the costs – monetary or otherwise – for patients, their families, and for society. On reflection, no one really accepts this proposal. Most people believe that quality of life can be so bad that death would be better. Some of them, faced with incurable illness and unavoidable suffering, request their own death.

But even if you are unmoved by this argument, there is another reason why the proposed solution cannot work. Even though our example for the aggregation problem concerned a treatment that prevented death, nothing turns on this. The aggregation problem can be reformulated without it. The problem remains if you try to compare, say, curing many mild headaches to preventing a serious and permanent disability (for instance, quadriplegia). On any aggregative view, it remains true that there is a sufficiently great number of people who can be given a smaller benefit such that their overall benefit outweighs the overall benefits for a few people, each of whom would receive a great benefit. The idea remains counterintuitive.

Consequently, we are back to the original problem. There is, however, another approach to the difficulty posed by the aggregation problem and the number problem. It is to introduce randomized decision procedures.

5.3 Fair chances

So far, we have considered two courses of action in the rescue case: preventing the greater number of deaths, and flipping a coin. Defenders of the aggregation thesis support the former. Critics of the aggregation thesis seem to have to support the latter. If you do not want to accept the aggregation thesis, but at the same time you want to take the numbers into account, there is the third option: to use a *weighted lottery*.

A weighted lottery is a randomized decision procedure. In the rescue case, you could assign a $5/6$ chance of being saved to the group of five people and a $1/6$ chance to the one person. The idea behind this randomized procedure is as follows. Each one of the six people has an equally strong moral claim to the good that you have to allocate. That good in the rescue case is having one's death averted. Ideally, you should divide the good equally among the six people. They all have an equally strong claim to it, so this is what fairness requires. However, the rescue case stipulates that you cannot reach everyone. The good cannot be distributed equally. But there is one thing that you can divide equally. That is the *chance* of getting the good.

So you divide the chance of being saved by the number of affected people. That number is six, so you give a $1/6$ chance to each one of the six people. $1/6$ is a *fair chance*. Of course, you still have to choose whether you save the one person or the five people. But now you assign the one person a $1/6$ chance. However, although each one of the five people also receives a $1/6$ chance, in practice their $1/6$ chance is pooled and increased from $1/6$ to $5/6$. Why? Suppose one of the five people wins the lottery. You will save that person. But you find four other people alongside, and you have a duty to save these four people. Surely, you cannot leave these four people unattended. Consequently, you assign a $5/6$ chance to the group of five people on the one hand, and a $1/6$ chance to the one person, on the other. With this weighted lottery, it is highly likely that you end up preventing the deaths of the five people.

A weighted lottery has four attractive features. First, it is sensitive to the numbers, but it also recognizes the moral claim of each one of the affected people. If the choice is between saving six people and saving one person, a weighted lottery gives $6/7$ chance to the six people and $1/7$ chance to the one person. The presence of each person really does make a difference to how you ought to proceed. But the way the numbers matter in a weighted lottery is different from the aggregation thesis.

Second, weighted lotteries do not rule out aggregation. Adding up the chances assigned to each one of the five people is evidently not inconsistent with the aggregation thesis. But again, unlike the straightforward maximization of benefits, a weighted lottery gives weight to the moral claims of all affected people.

Third, insofar as the chance of being saved is concerned, using a weighted lottery is a lot less extreme than simply saving the greater number. Suppose you adopt the policy of saving the greater number.

In the case of saving one person or one other person, you would give a 50 percent chance to each person. Now suppose that another person is added to one of the sides. The choice becomes between saving two people and saving one person. If you just go ahead and save the two, the chance of the one person is reduced from one half to zero. You might think this change is too radical. If you adopt a weighted lottery, in contrast, the presence of the additional person reduces the one person's chance of being saved from $1/2$ to $1/3$. The presence of an additional person does not affect the chance too radically.

Fourth, a weighted lottery offers you peace of mind. Even if there are some people whom you cannot save – perhaps the one person, perhaps the group of five – their fate was decided by the result of the lottery, over which you do not have any control. If you choose to save the five lives outright because of the general principle of saving the greater number, you may well end up with rescuer's guilt for the person you did not choose to save. With the weighted lottery, you can sleep easy.

Weighted lotteries may seem attractive in many contexts. One example might be the selection of recipients in organ transplants. When an organ becomes available, a list of possible recipients could be made, taking into account the health risks to each of them. Then, each patient's chance of receiving the organ could be determined by various factors such as age, time spent on the waiting list, prospective quality of life, and so on. A lottery might be used to determine the recipient. Under this procedure, every patient on the list has a chance to receive the organ.

Nevertheless, even though there might be some contexts in which weighted lotteries are attractive, they should not be accepted in the rescue case and many other cases. The main idea behind a weighted lottery is that the chances of getting an indivisible good should be distributed in a fair way. If you accept this idea, you should respect the distribution of chances regardless of the result of the lottery draw. Therefore, in the rescue case, if one of the five people is the winner of your lottery, you should save her alone and let the other four people die – even though you could save them as well.

This is because it is only one of the five people who won. If you save all the five people in this group, the original equal division of the chances will be overridden. Granted, it sounds counterintuitive not to save the four people when one of the five individuals wins her fair chance to be saved. But that is precisely the point. This is the price you have to pay to comply with the equal division of chances. Without respecting the chances assigned to each person throughout, you cannot maintain the equal distribution of chances among people with equally strong moral claims.

Suppose you give a $1/6$ chance to each person, and that one of the five people wins the lottery. Then, it might be argued that you have a moral obligation to save the other four people, even if you headed for the direction of the five people in order to save the winner only. This is because you can save the other four people without any additional cost or risk. Thus, it might be claimed that the equal division of chances practically entails the weighted lottery.

But this is odd. The rescue case presupposes that you save either the five people or the one person. When you decide to head for either direction, you already know whom you will save. If you head for the direction of the five, you already know that you will save all of them. If there is a moral obligation to save the remaining four people, it must be part of your moral argument that determines what you do. It must be present before, and not only after, you start moving in one direction.

We have suggested that if you stick to the original motivation for the weighted lottery – that is, the equal division of chances – you should waste the $1/6$ chance given to the other four people. You should let them die. But surely, it is a pity to waste the $1/6$ chance given to each one of these people. If you want to respect the equal distribution of chances, you should not pool the baseline chances of the five individuals. Rather, you should give an equal and *maximum* chance to each person. That is, you should increase the chance of each person up to $1/2$. This division gives an equal and maximal chance to each person.

Of course, now you are back at the coin-flipping proposal. So you face a dilemma. On the one hand, if you want to divide chances by the number of people and give an equal chance to each person, you should, ultimately, waste the chances of some people in order to comply with your initial argument for dividing the chance equally by the number of people. In practice, you might end up in a situation where you should not save some people, even though you are in a position to do so. This seems objectionable. On the other hand, if you want to give an equal and maximal chance to each person, each of them with an equally strong moral claim, then you should give each a $1/2$ chance, rather than drawing a weighted lottery. But we have already noted the difficulties for this proposal. It is objectionable too. Ultimately, we are led back to the aggregation thesis.

All in all, we believe the motivation behind weighted lotteries is mostly psychological. Their proponents want to show a clear sign of recognition to the moral claims of each person – including the one person in the rescue case – but at the bottom of their heart, they are hoping that the lottery result would not tell them to save the one person. It is highly unlikely that they end up with having to save the one person and let the five people die. If the lottery result forced them to save the one, they would feel a strong sense of regret – a regret they would not feel if the result was in favor of the greater number. Psychologically, we suspect, they just want to avoid a difficult decision. This psychology is perfectly understandable if you are not concerned with moral judgment. But it is not tenable when you are concerned with ethics. Ethics must offer coherent and justifiable arguments that help responsible people make difficult decisions. If you hope to get away from difficult decisions by using chances, you will also avoid hard moral judgments. In our view, randomized decision procedures should only be used in the cases when you must break a tie among people with equally strong claims to getting a good.

5.4 Choosing patients

The rescue case was a toy example – a thought experiment to help us formulate and examine moral principles about the distribution of benefits. But it was unlike most of the other examples that we have considered so far, since it involved the selection of the people who would receive some benefit. So far, we have been at pains to emphasize in this book that most of health care resource allocation concerns the selection of interventions, rather than the selection of people.

In exceptional cases, however, resource allocation choices involve the selection of patients. In the rescue case, we imagined that you have to decide who can live and who must die. For those exceptional cases when selection of patients is inevitable, our discussion has direct implications. We will consider three cases. In these examples, the principle of benefit maximization, and therefore the aggregation thesis, are taken for granted.

We already mentioned the first example in Chapter 4. It is triage, a selection procedure employed in mass-casualty incidents. In circumstances such as battles, train wrecks, natural disasters, or large-scale terrorist attacks, it may not be possible to save the lives of all victims. Under normal circumstances, many of the victims could be saved – or at least would be worthy of the best effort at life-saving. Triage allocates limited health care resources in a way that maximizes the number of lives saved. It focuses on those casualties for whom immediate medical attention makes the difference between life and death. They are given priority compared to those who will survive without immediate medical attention as well as those who are either unlikely to survive even with immediate attention or require more complex interventions than others.

The underlying idea is an extreme version of the aggregation thesis. In the case of triage, the health benefit that is aggregated is number of lives saved. The maximization of the number of lives saved is the primary and only goal, regardless of age, health-related quality of life, or other factors. Triage does not take into account who came first, either. If you reject the aggregation thesis and agree that the numbers should not affect what you ought to do, then it is perfectly sensible to treat the patient who came first and leave two patients to die whose lives could have been saved in the time you stabilize the first patient. But few people would agree with such a procedure in cases of extreme and acute resource scarcity.

The second example is a bit more complicated. It is the case of a pandemic influenza outbreak. If a large number of people are infected by the influenza, there may not be enough vaccines or ventilators. The resources may not be sufficient to meet the needs of all people. It is unlikely that the necessary amount of vaccines can be stockpiled or enough ventilators can be installed in advance. In that case, it would be inevitable, at least for some time, to leave some people untreated and with the risk of dying.

In the case of the global swine flu outbreak in 2009, health authorities around the world encountered this difficult problem. Canada was one of the few countries that had a sufficient amount of vaccines for each of its citizens. Other countries such as Japan, Sweden, and the United States did not. Health authorities in these countries had to select priority groups for vaccination. They decided that the highest priority should be given to health care workers such as physicians, nurses, and hospital technicians. In their absence, there would be no functioning health care system. This would be bad for everyone. Health authorities envisaged that as more vaccines become available, priority should then be given to high-risk groups such as aged people, pregnant women, young children, and people with chronic disease. The aim of this prioritization scheme would be to maximize the number of lives saved. From the perspective of public health, this makes sense, because one of the central missions of public health is to minimize premature mortality.

However, some people might argue that from the ethical point of view it is not obvious that you should aim for maximizing the number of lives saved and allocate vaccines and ventilators accordingly. Critics of the aggregation thesis might argue for a weighted lottery. For example, you could give one lottery ticket to individuals in low-risk groups, two tickets to people with chronic disease, 20 tickets to health care workers, and so on. The number of tickets given to each person would be determined by the degree of exposure to risk. In the case of a pandemic outbreak, you could then conduct a lottery draw and announce the winning ticket numbers. People with these tickets would have access to vaccines first.

This version of a weighted lottery gives some chance of vaccination to everyone. But those who are exposed to a greater risk of infection or death have a greater chance of getting the vaccination than those who are exposed to a smaller risk. This method of vaccine distribution does not aim to maximize the number of lives saved. It may well fail to save many lives that could have been saved if you opted for benefit maximization. So, this method might appear unpractical and unrealistic to health care policymakers. But, from the ethical point of view, you cannot take benefit maximization for granted. The fact that it appears obvious in public health does not entail that it is ethically defensible. There still must be an ethical case for it – like the arguments we have provided in this chapter.

The selection of people also crops up in the context of implementing preventive policies. For instance, alcohol-related health problems are a major concern in many societies. Suppose you want to reduce the health risks associated with alcohol consumption by introducing some new policy. Whom should you target with your measures? Obviously, you would not target those who never drink; you would target those who are in some high-risk group for alcohol-related health problems.

But this might not be the best strategy. A small reduction of the risks among the large number of moderate-risk, moderate drinkers can result in a greater reduction of the burden of disease due to alcohol consumption than a greater reduction of the risks among the fewer high-risk heavy drinkers. This might be because the incidence of alcohol-related health problems is greater among the larger group even if each person in this group has a much smaller individual risk. Paradoxically, even though it might seem that the best policy is that which targets high-risk individuals, each of who could each greatly benefit, it might in fact be better to target low-risk individuals, each of whose expected benefits are much smaller. This is known as the *prevention paradox*. It arises in all sorts of preventive policies, from the fluoridation of the water supply to antenatal screening programs.

Of course, the prevention paradox is not really a paradox to those who accept the aggregation thesis. They are prepared to accept that small benefits to a large number of people can outweigh greater benefits to a few. They are prepared to accept that the burden of a disease might be best reduced by targeting those who are less likely to suffer from that disease. The paradox is more troubling for those who reject aggregation. They have to insist that the greater benefits to the few cannot be traded off for greater overall benefits. For those who reject aggregation, it is difficult to take a population-level perspective. But from this perspective, the paradox disappears.

5.5 Giving priority to the worse off

Let us go back to the example of appendectomy and tooth capping. Many people find ranking tooth capping above appendectomy counterintuitive. One explanation for their intuitive judgment was the alleged implausibility of the aggregation thesis. But, as we saw, the theoretical cost of giving up the aggregation thesis is huge.

Here is another possible explanation. A patient with appendectomy is more seriously ill than a patient with a toothache. A benefit to a more seriously ill patient should receive a greater moral weight than a benefit to a less seriously ill patient, even if the benefits are of equal size. Improving the condition of a more seriously ill patient is more important.

On the principle of benefit maximization, QALYs are aggregated by simply adding them up. If you aggregate QALYs this way, the only thing that matters is their sum. It does not matter how they are distributed between different people.

Consider the following example. There are two patients. Patient A is more seriously ill than Patient B. A's health-related quality of life level is 0.4; B's is 0.7. We represent this state of affairs by writing (0.4, 0.7). The first number is the outcome for A; the second number is the outcome for B.

You can improve the condition of one – and only one – patient by 0.2. So your choice is between X = (0.6, 0.7) and Y = (0.4, 0.9). If you simply add up the values in the outcomes, X and Y are equally good because their sums are the same. However, it could be argued that X is better than Y. Why? Because the level of the worse off is improved in X. Given that the health improvements are of the same size, it is better to treat the worse off rather than the better off: the benefit to the worse off person counts more than the benefit to the better off person.

It is possible to incorporate this idea into the process of QALY aggregation. You can assign a greater weight to the benefits of the worse off. Here is one distributive principle, which has become known as *prioritarianism*. According to prioritarianism, you should give greater weight to benefiting the worse off and add up the weighted well-being across different individuals. More precisely, on prioritarianism, the overall goodness of a state of affairs is an increasing, strictly concave function of people's well-being.[1]

An increasing, strictly concave function is the one that is strictly increasing but bends downwards. That is, its value increases as its arguments increase, but at a decreasing rate. A graphical example is given on the right-hand side of Figure 3.1 in Chapter 3. Another example is a square-root function.

Weighting benefits by an increasing and strictly concave function assigns greater value to the same benefit to the worse off than to the better off. The value of an increase in a better off person's well-being is strictly smaller than the value of the same increase in a worse off person's well-being. The value of a person's well-being is interpreted as its *moral value*. According to prioritarianism, the goodness of a state of affairs is determined by the weighted sum of people's well-being. The weights determine the moral value of people's well-being. Evidently, prioritarianism is an aggregative view: it determines the value of an outcome by adding up the moral value of people's well-being.

In Chapter 3, we discussed equity weighting. Assigning equity weights to QALYs (or other measures of health benefit) can be interpreted as an application of prioritarianism to the allocation of health care resources.

On this view, the goodness of a health care resource allocation is judged by the weighted sum of people's QALYs. Here, what is aggregated is not overall well-being, but only one component of it. This is why "QALY prioritarianism" is a practical application of the general moral principle.

For an illustration, consider the example we began with. You can improve the health-related quality of life of patient A or B by 0.2 for one year. The two possible outcomes are X = (0.6, 0.7) and Y = (0.4, 0.9). Thus, in X, Patient A receives 0.2 QALYs, and Patient B remains at 0.7. In Y, Patient B gets 0.2 QALYs, and A remains at 0.4.

One way to aggregate QALYs is to take their unweighted sum. In this case, X is just as good as Y because the unweighted sum is 1.3 in both X and Y. However, according to prioritarianism, X is strictly better than Y. If we choose X instead of Y, Patient A's condition will improve by 0.2. If we choose Y instead of X, Patient B's condition will improve by 0.2. According to prioritarianism, given that the health-related quality of life of Patient A is lower than that of Patient B, the moral value of providing 0.2 QALYs to Patient A is greater than the moral value of providing the same QALY improvement to Patient B. (You can check this by taking the square root function as an example. Verify that $\sqrt{0.6} + \sqrt{0.7} > \sqrt{0.4} + \sqrt{0.9}$).

Given this prioritarian function, a QALY to a worse off person counts for more than a QALY to a better off person. If you aggregate QALYs with a strictly concave function, the aggregated moral value of the QALYs in X is strictly greater than in Y.

In Chapter 4, we introduced another possible application of prioritarianism – this time, to life years. We showed how an age-weighting function with a prioritarian form can account for the fair innings argument. Figure 4.1 on page 94 illustrates both utilitarian and prioritarian "ageism." We will not go through the details here again.

Prioritarianism is egalitarian in a certain sense. When the sum of QALYs are equal, a more equal distribution is better than a less equal one. But prioritarianism is different from egalitarianism in one important sense. It avoids what has become known as the *leveling down objection* to egalitarianism.

Let us first explain egalitarianism. Egalitarians usually accept at least two principles. First, and most importantly, they accept the *principle of equality*. According to this principle, it is in itself bad if some people are worse off than others. However, the principle of equality alone cannot be a plausible distributive principle. Imagine two states of affairs with two individuals: (0.5, 0.5) and (1.0, 1.0). The two states exhibit perfect equality. If equality is the only relevant principle, then you must hold that these two states are equally good. But (1.0, 1.0) must be better than (0.5, 0.5), because everyone is better off in it. So the principle of equality should be combined with another principle. That principle could say, for example, that it is in itself better if people are better off. When the principle of equality is combined with this principle, it does not follow that (1.0, 1.0) is not better than (0.5, 0.5). By egalitarianism, we refer to a class of views that accept the principle of equality and some principle that ensures this implication.

Now, back to the leveling down objection. The general form of the objection runs as follows. Egalitarianism holds that it is bad if some people are worse off than others. But suppose that the level of well-being of a better off person is lowered to the level of well-being of a worse off person. No one benefits from this: the worse off person's level of well-being is not increased. Call this "leveling down". Egalitarianism must judge that the leveling down is, at least in one respect, strictly better: it makes the outcome more equal. But, according to the leveling down objection, the leveling down is not better in any respect. Thus, the objection concludes that egalitarianism is absurd.

For illustration, consider the following two outcomes: X = (0.9, 0.6) and Y = (0.6, 0.6). If you move from X to Y, it is an instance of leveling down. Is Y better than X in any respect? According to the objection, egalitarianism must judge that Y is *better in one respect* than X, because there is perfect equality in Y. But many people would think that there is nothing good about moving from X to Y. That is why egalitarianism is absurd.

The issue of the leveling down occasionally crops up in real-life contexts. In Chapter 3, we referred to the controversy of "topping up" in the United Kingdom. It used to be the case that patients lost their eligibility for treatment within the National Health Service if they paid out-of-pocket for medicines that were not available because of their unfavorable cost-effectiveness ratio. But when some patients pay for expensive medicines from their own resources, it does not worsen the situation of those who cannot afford to pay. Prohibiting topping up made some patients worse off without making anyone better off. Thus, the prohibition of topping up can be seen as an instance of leveling down.

In the eyes of the defenders of the prohibition of topping up, it is unfair if rich patients can get expensive medicines that poor patients cannot. Thus, according to these critics, leveling down can be justified in this context. Their opponents, in contrast, argue that there is no unfairness if rich patients can get expensive medicines without burdening the health care system or worsening the quality of the treatment of other patients. They even argue that the prohibition of topping up is unfair to those who can afford to pay. They contend that leveling down is hard to accept.

Prioritarianism is not vulnerable to the leveling down objection. Leveling down is not better in any respect. Thus, prioritarianism avoids the objection but captures some egalitarian motivation by giving priority to the worse off. In recent years, many philosophers have come to support prioritarianism, rather than egalitarianism. If you believe that benefiting the worse off is important, one way to go is to adopt prioritarianism. But this means that you do not reject the aggregation thesis. Although you give greater priority to benefits to the worse off, smaller benefits to many people who are better off can still lead to a better outcome. If you have to choose between appendectomy and tooth cappings, providing tooth cappings to many patients will be better, provided that the number of people who require tooth capping is sufficiently large. Thus, you cannot entirely avoid the counterintuitive implication of the aggregation thesis. But you can reduce it.

Hence prioritarianism is not the perfect solution. At the same time, perhaps there is no perfect solution. Prioritarianism seems to be the least unacceptable solution to the aggregation problem.

Nevertheless, a full defense of prioritarianism would require answering further questions.

One question is this: How much priority should be given to the worse off? The most extreme version of the idea of giving priority to the worse off is *leximin*, an extension of what is known as the *maximin* rule. We need to explain these rules. Let us begin with maximin. This rule determines the relative goodness of distributions by considering the level of the worst off. For example, compare $X = (0.6, 0.7)$ and $Y = (0.4, 0.9)$. According to maximin, X is strictly better than Y, because the level of the worst off in X (0.6) is higher than in Y (0.4). For maximin, nothing else matters. Thus, in comparing $X = (0.6, 0.7)$ and $Z = (0.6, 0.9)$, maximin judges that X is just good as Z. The rule considers only the level of the worst off. This judgment is very counterintuitive, because Z is strictly better for the second person and no worse for the first person. Because of this feature, very few people accept maximin.

Leximin is the lexicographic extension of maximin. When you use a dictionary to find the meaning of a word, say "ethics," you first look for the pages where the words starting with "e" are collected. You then look for the pages where the second letter is "t" among the words starting with "e," and the pages where the third letter is "h," and so on. Leximin determines the ranking of outcomes in a similar way to the ordering of words in a dictionary. Like maximin, leximin first compares the outcomes for the worst off in different distributions. But when the level of the worst off is the same in all distributions, it compares the outcomes for the second worst off. When the level of the second worst off is the same in all distributions, it compares the outcomes of the third worst off. And so on. Thus, leximin judges that Z is strictly better than X, because the level of the worst off is the same but the level of the second worst off in Z is higher than in X. Thus, leximin avoids the counterintuitive implication of maximin.

Leximin gives absolute priority to the worst off over the less worse off, and if all outcomes are equally good for the worst off, it gives absolute priority to the second worst off, and so on. Just like the maximin rule, however, leximin has an extreme implication. It stems from the fact that leximin does not satisfy the aggregation thesis. According to the rule, any gain to the worst off, no matter how small, outweighs any loss to other people, no matter how great. To see this, compare the following distributions:

S = (0.4, 0.6, 0.6, 0.6, 0.6)

T = (0.4, 0.5, 0.9, 0.9, 0.9)

According to leximin, S is strictly better than T because while the level of the worst off in S and T are the same (0.4), the level of the second-worst off in S (0.6) is higher than in T (0.5). However, T is not worse than S for anyone except the second person: it is equally good for the first person, and strictly better for everyone else. The problem is that leximin does not allow the aggregation of benefits and losses. On this rule, any small gain for the worse off, no matter how small, can justify a great loss for the better off – regardless of the number of people who would suffer that loss. This counterintuitive implication, which directly follows from the rejection of the aggregation thesis, leads to what is known in health care resource allocation as the *bottomless pit problem*: benefiting the worse off "swallows up" all resources from everybody who is better off. (We already appealed to this problem in our argument against the disability discrimination objection on page 87.) For this reason, many people are opposed to giving absolute priority to the worse off. Prioritarianism can avoid the bottomless pit problem if it is formulated in a way that satisfies the aggregation thesis. Our formulation above does this, because even though it gives some priority to the worse off, it does not give absolute priority.

This point leads to our second question. Who is the worse off? Surprisingly, it is difficult to answer this simple question. In the appendectomy/tooth capping case, it is easy to identify the worse off. Obviously, patients with appendicitis are worse off than patients with toothache. Why? Because they are more severely ill. Should the worse off then be defined as the most severely ill? Not necessarily. There are at least three other senses in which a patient can be worse off.

First, a person who has been ill for a longer period of time may be considered worse off than a person who has been ill for a shorter time, even if these two people are equally severely ill at the moment. Suppose there are two patients, A and B, with the exact same condition. Both can derive the same health improvement from an intervention. The only difference between the two patients is that A has been suffering from the condition for many years, whereas B has only recently developed it. Intuitively, A is worse off than B, simply because A has been suffering for a longer period.

However, if you focus only on their prospective health-related quality of life without the intervention, A and B are equally badly off, since their expected health outcome is the same. In principle, the aggregation of health benefits is forward-looking. It does not consider what has happened in the past.

In practice, there are ways to take past health into consideration in health care resource allocation. One example is waiting lists. In the example, a waiting list can serve as a way to take into account past health: since A has been ill for longer, she is higher up on the waiting list for the intervention. At the population level, the length of waiting lists can be taken into account – for example, areas where waiting lists are longer can be allocated more resources. Note, however, that using waiting lists as a way to give consideration to past health is not entailed by benefit maximization. Past health is an additional consideration.

Second, a person may be considered worse off when and because her condition could see little improvement. For example, patients with severe chronic obstructive pulmonary disease or with severe chronic schizophrenia are largely resistant to standard pharmacological treatments. The severity of their conditions makes them very badly off. But the fact that they can expect little improvement makes their fate even worse. It makes perfect sense to think that those who can expect little improvement in their condition are truly worst off.

The third sense in which a person may be considered worse off is in terms of overall well-being. Suppose that a concert pianist gets one of her fingers injured. Her career as a concert pianist comes to an end because of the injury. A finger injury is unlikely to be serious or life-threatening as a medical condition, but it is extremely serious for the pianist. It seriously affects her overall well-being.

Our application of prioritarianism to the allocation of health care resources – what we might call, for lack of a better label, the principle of "QALY prioritarianism" – does not consider overall well-being. It takes account only of health-related quality of life. The aggregation of QALYs, no matter how you go about it, does not capture any value beyond the value of health. This may be no bad thing. You can argue that the goal of health care and health policy is to promote population health, not overall well-being. It is a matter for broader social and public policy to promote people's overall well-being. It makes sense to confine health care and health policy to health-related quality of life. We take up this issue in the next chapter.

Chapter summary

Maximizing health benefits presupposes the aggregation thesis and, in particular, its implication that small benefits to a large number of people can outweigh large benefits to a few. It may be argued that no such trade-offs should be allowed and priority should be given to those who are worse off, regardless of the number of beneficiaries. However, the rejection of the aggregation thesis comes at a very high price: without the thesis, it is difficult to justify the case for saving the greater number of people in the rescue case. But the concern for the worse off can be reconciled with the aggregation thesis if prioritarianism is adopted. We have shown how prioritarianism can be applied in the context of health care resource allocation. Nonetheless, there remains the problem of identifying the worse off in this context.

Discussion questions

1. The rejection of the aggregation thesis leads us to the number problem, but it is difficult to solve the number problem without appealing to the aggregation thesis. This is one reason for accepting the aggregation thesis. But this is a negative reason. Are there any positive reasons for accepting the aggregation thesis?
2. In the 2009 H1N1 flu (or "swine flu") pandemic, many countries did not have a sufficient amount of vaccines stockpiled. They had to set priorities between different patient groups. In the United Kingdom, for example, the groups with the highest priority included (1) people aged between 6 months and 65 years who have underlying health conditions, (2) pregnant women, (3) people who live with patients with compromised immune systems, (4) people aged over 65 with underlying health conditions, and (5) frontline health workers. However, healthy children were not given priority even though they are widely recognized as major "virus-spreaders."[2] Can such a policy be justified? How?
3. Imagine you have to choose recipients from a waiting list for kidney transplants by using a lottery. Would you use a weighted or unweighted lottery? If you would choose a weighted lottery, what sorts of factors should determine the weights?
4. We discussed several different accounts of what it is to be worse off. Which account is the most acceptable? Why? Are there any other possible accounts?
5. If we accept the aggregation thesis, do we have to countenance picking one healthy person randomly, harvesting their organs and transplanting them to five needy patients? If not, why not?

Further readings

The philosophical debate on aggregation starts with Taurek (1977). Its implications for the allocation of health care resources are discussed in a symposium by Daniels *et al.* (1994). For a comprehensive study on the aggregation problem and the number problem, read Hirose (2014*b*). The principle of pairwise comparison is put forward by Nagel (1979). The tie-breaking argument is due to Scanlon (1998, ch. 5). For the possibility of a lottery in recipient selection for organ transplantation, see Brock (1988). Verweij (2009) offers a clear assessment of the ethical issues arising from rationing health care resources during an influenza pandemic; see also Peterson (2008). In philosophy, prioritarianism was introduced by Parfit (1995). Its application to health care resource allocation is discussed by Brock (2002*b*). For an introduction to egalitarianism and other distributive principles, see Hirose (2014*a*) and Tungodden (2003).

Notes

1 More formally, prioritarianism is the view that a state of affairs, $X = (w_1, w_2, \ldots, w_n)$, is at least as good as another, $Y = (w'_1, w'_2, \ldots, w'_n)$, if and only if $f(w_1) + f(w_2) + \ldots + f(w_n) \geq f(w'_1) + f(w'_2) + \ldots + f(w'_n)$, where w_i denotes the well-being level of person i and $f(.)$ is some increasing, strictly concave function. It is not difficult to read this definition. X and Y are outcomes or states of affairs described by the levels of well-being, w, of all the affected people, listed in the subscript from 1 to n. The value of X and Y is determined by each person's level of well-being, weighted by a function f. The arguments of the function are levels of well-being. They are modified by the function to express their moral value.

2 See "Healthy children and over 65s are not swine flu vaccine priority." *The Telegraph*, August 13, 2009, http://www.telegraph.co.uk/health/swine-flu/6023403/Healthy-children-and-over-65s-are-not-swine-flu-vaccine-priority.html.

6   Responsibility for health

6.1 Equality and luck

So far, we have focused on the allocation of resources in health care. In this final chapter, we will broaden the scope of our discussion. We will consider the distribution of health, rather than the distribution of health care only. We will go beyond considering only health-related quality of life for the evaluation of resource allocations.

Focusing only on health-related quality of life has intuitive appeal. In this "health-only" framework, the allocation of health care resources is determined solely by health benefits, excluding other characteristics. For example, suppose that two patients are brought into the emergency room. You can treat only one of them. The expected health benefits from treating either are the same. The only difference between the two patients is that one is a millionaire and the other is a poor person. If you focus only on health-related quality of life, you should not give priority to either of these patients.

This is as it should be. The professional duty of health care workers is to focus on restoring and maintaining their patients' health, not on considering, for instance, how important a millionaire is for the economy. Every person's life has equal worth, and everyone's health should be equally important.

Thus, the morally appropriate basis for setting priorities in health care is the maintenance and promotion of the population's health. Factors like economic contribution should not affect judgments about health care resource allocation. In this respect, it is intuitively appealing and ethically defensible to focus on patients' health alone, and to intentionally ignore other, non-health-related factors – such as income, level of education, social status, gender, race, sexual orientation, and so on.

However, some people argue that this seemingly plausible feature of the health-only framework can simultaneously be a disadvantage. They contend that there are some ethical issues that are missing from it. These ethical issues arise from the connection between health outcomes and individual behavior, as well as health outcomes and socioeconomic background. If you focus on health-related quality of life only, you miss these connections. But they are morally relevant.

Health outcomes and individual behavior are closely connected when it comes to risk factors such as smoking, obesity, excess drinking, unsafe sex, and so on. Many people would agree that individual responsibility for minimizing these risk factors should be taken into account in priority setting in health care. But, as we shall show, health outcomes are also indirectly connected to socioeconomic factors that themselves affect these risk factors. Thus, some people make an even stronger claim. They contend that even though smoking or obesity is the cause of disease, broader socioeconomic factors are the *causes* of the causes of disease. How these direct and indirect factors should be taken into account in health care resource allocation is a very difficult question.

Let us begin with an example of smoking. Suppose that two patients develop heart disease and require a heart transplant to continue to live. Let us assume that the only difference between the two patients is their past lifestyles. Patient A was a heavy smoker for 20 years, but he quit smoking several years prior to developing heart disease, and since then he has been committed to a healthy lifestyle. Patient B, in contrast, never smoked, ate a balanced diet his entire life, and exercised regularly. Suppose also that the expected health benefit from the heart transplant would be the same for both patients, given that A has lived a healthy life for several years since quitting smoking.

The health-only framework holds that insofar as the health benefits are the same, these two patients should be treated in exactly the same way. If only one heart is available for transplant, perhaps you should flip a fair coin to decide who should receive it. If only health-related quality of life should be considered, there is no morally relevant difference between the two patients.

Many people disagree with this reply. They argue that there is one important difference between A and B, even if there is no difference in their health conditions and expected health benefits. The difference is that A's health need is a consequence of his own behavior. For the sake of the argument, we shall assume that this is indeed the case. Despite quitting years ago, A's past behavior is the cause of his health condition. Thus, some people argue, given that A has a history of smoking, he should be held responsible, at least in part, for developing heart disease. Patient B, in contrast, is simply unlucky and should not be held responsible for his poor health. Therefore, you should give the heart transplant to B. This choice is justified by the difference in their responsibility.

To generalize the argument: many people think that there is a moral difference between health needs that patients could have avoided through healthy behavior, and those that they could not. If resources are scarce, then higher priority should be given to those who took good care of themselves by avoiding risky and harmful activities such as smoking, excess consumption of junk food, binge drinking, needle-sharing, dangerous sports, unprotected casual sex, and so on.

If responsibility should play any role at all in health care resource allocation, what kind of ethical principle can allow it to do so? There is a philosophical position that captures many people's intuition in the case of the two heart disease patients. It is called *luck egalitarianism*.

To explain luck egalitarianism, we must first introduce a distinction between two kinds of luck. In the case of the two heart disease patients, A chose an unhealthy lifestyle even though he knew that smoking increases the risk of developing serious diseases such as lung cancer and cardiovascular disease. It is true that some heavy smokers do not develop these diseases and live healthy and long lives. So Patient A is, in a sense, unlucky for developing heart disease. His bad health condition is the result of bad luck. Patient B, on the other hand, chose a healthy lifestyle but, as a result of bad luck, developed heart disease. Some non-smokers develop heart disease. So B is also unlucky. His bad health condition is a result of bad luck as well. However, there is a morally relevant difference between A's bad luck and B's bad luck. Patient A could have reduced his chances of developing heart disease if he opted for a healthy lifestyle. He had freedom of choice and exercised it. He intentionally chose to smoke cigarettes, and his intentional choice of smoking increased his chance of developing heart disease. In B's case, by contrast, the effect of bad luck is unrelated to the person's choices. He did not have any control over his likelihood of developing heart disease. Let us call A's bad luck bad *option luck*, because A had the option to choose a healthy lifestyle and nonetheless chose to opt for a risky and potentially harmful one. Let us call B's bad luck bad *brute luck*.

In general terms, luck egalitarianism holds that inequality of well-being is unjust when and because it reflects the bad effects of brute luck. The effects of bad brute luck should be compensated *as a matter of justice*. But luck egalitarianism also claims that inequalities due to the effects of bad option luck are not unjust. They should not be compensated as a matter of justice. That is, if someone is worse off than another as a result of his or her own intentional choices, then this inequality does not give rise to any ethical concern.

Luck egalitarianism in health is, obviously, more specific. It holds that inequalities in health are unjust when and because they reflect the bad effects of brute luck (or when they reflect something other than choice). Luck egalitarianism in health is the view that it is unjust if some people are worse off than others in terms of health through no fault or choice of their own, and that as a matter of justice they should be compensated or helped to overcome the bad effects of brute luck. When their bad health is a result of brute luck, people should not be held responsible for its consequences. But luck egalitarianism in health also implies that it is not unjust if some people are worse off than others as a result of their intentional choices – for instance, as a result of their choice of lifestyle. As a matter of justice, society is not required to compensate or help people who suffer from the bad effects of option luck.

What does luck egalitarianism imply in the case of the two patients with heart disease?

On the one hand, Patient A developed heart disease as a result of bad luck. But his condition is a result of option luck – that is, luck that he himself triggered. Therefore, A should be held responsible for this consequence. Of course, some heavy smokers do not develop heart disease. But inequality in terms of health between A and other heavy smokers with no heart disease is justifiable. It is not a matter of justice. Patient B, on the other hand, also developed heart disease as a result of bad luck, but his condition is a result of bad brute luck, which he could not control. Therefore, according to luck egalitarianism, B should not be held responsible for the consequences of his luck. Of course, there are many people like B who choose healthy lifestyles, but, unlike B, do not develop heart disease. According to luck egalitarianism, the health inequality between B and these healthy people does give rise to an ethical concern. It is a matter of justice. It is just to compensate B for his bad health by, for example, giving higher priority to his treatment. Thus, given that the health conditions of A and B are the same, luck egalitarianism in health contends that it is not unjust to give priority to B over A when it comes to allocating scarce health care resources for heart disease treatment.

It is important to recognize that luck egalitarianism is not a view about what people deserve. Luck egalitarianism in health does not aim to track desert. Luck egalitarians do not claim that a patient like A deserves his bad health or that he deserves no health care. Rather, luck egalitarians aim to take individual responsibility seriously and offer it as a basis for setting priorities between different interventions and patients when resources are scarce. Theirs is not a view about desert.

To be sure, some extremists might claim that patients like A do not deserve heart transplants. But such claims are unwarranted by egalitarianism.

Furthermore, egalitarianism is not the only view that can take responsibility into account. At the end of the last chapter, we discussed prioritarianism. Some philosophers believe that prioritarianism is able to avoid some of the problems with egalitarianism – like the leveling down objection – and hence it is a better view of distributive justice. Prioritarianism can also be formulated as a responsibility-sensitive view. Such a view would hold, very roughly, that you should give higher priority to the benefits of those who are worse off and not responsible, through their own choices, for being worse off. This characterization is obviously rough and informal, because there are several distinct ways that prioritarians might wish to formulate the weighting of well-being that incorporates a measure of the degree of people's responsibility. We will not go into any details here. The point is simply that if you prefer prioritarianism to egalitarianism, and you also share the intuitions about responsibility, you can accept a *luck prioritarian* view. In the examples we are discussing, the two sorts of view would have the same implications. Luck egalitarians and luck prioritarians would agree, for instance, that Patient B should be given higher priority for a heart transplant than Patient A. Thus, to keep matters simple, we will continue to focus on luck egalitarianism.

It seems that many people share the intuition that you should give priority to Patient B over A when you cannot provide heart transplants to both. Luck egalitarianism (or luck prioritarianism) captures this intuition fairly well. Well, at least at first glance. But some of the theoretical implications of these views are far from intuitively plausible. Here is one. Some people die young through no fault of their own, and other people live long. This is an unfortunate fact. But does this fact give rise to any ethical concern? Is it a *matter of justice*? According to luck egalitarianism, it is. It is unjust if some people die young when it is a consequence of bad brute luck. But is this plausible?

This is not obviously clear. We are certainly sympathetic to those who die young as a result of bad brute luck – say, an incurable genetic disease. Their death is a tragedy. Many people also feel as though it is, in a sense, unfair. But this is not the sort of unfairness for which anybody could be held responsible. It is not a consequence of anybody's decisions or actions. Nor is it a consequence of any collective action, government policy, or social system. The mere fact that some people die young through no fault of their own is not a matter of justice – even if it is unfair, in a cosmic sense, in the great scheme of things. But luck egalitarianism implies that when someone dies younger than others purely as a result of bad brute luck, there is a different, social form of unfairness that gives rise to the concern for justice.

There is, however, a more serious, unattractive implication of luck egalitarianism. Consider the following example. A reckless motorcyclist with no insurance collides with another motorcyclist who always drives carefully and purchases insurance each year. Both motorcyclists are severely injured. Luck egalitarianism implies that there is nothing objectionable about offering treatment to the careful motorcyclist only and refusing treatment to the reckless motorcyclist, even if there are sufficient resources left after the careful motorcyclist is treated. The inequality between the reckless motorcyclist and the careful motorcyclist is not unjust, since the reckless motorcyclist is worse off through his own fault. Of course, the reckless motorcyclist did not choose to collide. But he can be reasonably expected to drive carefully and purchase insurance, which he did not do. Hence, we should not be concerned, as a matter of justice, to provide treatment to him. He has no claim of justice on us for assistance. But, to many people, this implication of luck egalitarianism is unjustifiably harsh. It seems that the view condones abandoning people who are responsible for their bad luck. This is the *abandonment objection* to luck egalitarianism.

There are several ways defenders of luck egalitarianism in health can try to meet this objection. They can point out that, strictly speaking, their view does not entail that you should never give any treatment to those who are responsible for their health care need. Luck egalitarianism entails merely that it is not unjust to give *relative* priority to those whose health care need is a result of bad brute luck compared to those whose need is a result of bad option luck. True, you should give priority to treating the careful motorcyclist. But if there were enough resources and time, you should not abandon the reckless motorcyclist either. If there was no scarcity of resources, the view would not imply that it would be unjust to address health care needs that are the result of bad option luck and withhold care from those who are responsible for their misfortune. So the view applies only when priorities must be set between health care resources that are scarce. It is not as harsh as it looks.

Even so, this reply is not entirely satisfactory. For it remains the case that treating the reckless motorcyclist is not a matter of justice, even when there are enough resources. The motorcyclist has no moral claims on society's resources. And this does sound harsh: it still considers helping him optional from the point of view of justice. But probably few would want to defend the view that helping people is optional in this sense, even when they are responsible for their misfortune. Who among us has never done anything reckless or stupid?

Some proponents of luck egalitarianism attempt to respond to the abandonment objection in a different way. Here is their argument. Although luck egalitarianism itself does allow abandoning the reckless motorcyclist, proponents of luck egalitarianism should not accept or recommend abandoning him. This is because proponents of luck egalitarianism are allowed to support multiple moral principles simultaneously. Other moral principles do demand doing as much as possible to save the life of the reckless motorcyclist. These other moral principles may be principles based on charity, solidarity, beneficence, humanism, and so on. Consequently, even though luck egalitarianism does abandon the reckless motorcyclist, one or more of the other principles would require helping him. According to this response, luck egalitarianism is a principle of distributive justice, which is only one part of moral theory.

Luck egalitarians have a broader moral view, other parts of which will mitigate the harshness of their view on distributive justice. This reply could be called the *pluralist response*.

The pluralist response, however, is unsatisfactory for two reasons. First, the worry about harshness still applies to luck egalitarianism. The response under consideration concedes that luck egalitarianism itself abandons the reckless motorcyclist, and that luck egalitarianism itself offers no reason for saving his life. Therefore, luck egalitarianism itself remains unjustifiably harsh. Second, the response concedes that luck egalitarianism is not a comprehensive moral principle for the distribution of burdens and bene- fits – even though it is proposed as a principle of distributive justice. Luck egalitarianism, applied to health care or other areas of social policy, is only a partial principle. But whether reckless or imprudent people are owed full, partial, or no assistance is one of the most fundamental and important questions in distributive justice. What moral claims people have on others is the basic question of justice, and that question includes what is owed to people who are responsible for their misfortune. Luck egalitarianism itself gives a negative answer to this fundamental question in distributive justice, but it expects that its negative answer will be overridden by other moral considerations. That is a decidedly odd position to take.

There is a final worry about luck egalitarianism that must be raised. It is not so much an objection as an observation. In the writings of luck egalitarians, you regularly encounter a familiar cast of characters: reckless motorcyclists, heavy smokers who need heart transplants, former alco- holics who need new livers, daredevil mountaineers who ignore storm warnings. They are contrasted with careful motorcyclists, non-smokers with heart disease, teetotalers with liver failure, innocent schoolchildren out in the mountains on a class trip. Indeed, we have used some of these characters ourselves.

Yet in the arguments of luck egalitarians you hardly ever meet mara- thon runners who need knee replacements as a consequence of years of running on hard surfaces, stressed out single mothers holding down multiple jobs and trying to raise children, or people who test the limits of human endurance in order to raise money for charity. Few luck egalitar- ians advertise their view by arguing that professional women who post- pone having their first child until their late thirties should have lower priority for breast cancer treatment than women who had their first child in their early twenties. Yet postponing childbearing until the late thirties doubles a woman's risk of breast cancer compared to those who have their first child in their early twenties.

The worry this observation raises is that our intuitions about responsi- bility might in part reflect social ideas about acceptable and objectionable behavior, or even prejudice. In a famous study, respondents were asked to allocate heart transplants between patients with and without a history of intravenous drug use, patients with and without a history of cigarette smoking, and patients with and without a history of eating a high-fat diet against their doctors' recommendation. Not surprisingly, there was a strong relationship between patients' past behavior and the willingness of respondents to provide them with heart transplants: compared to people with no history of risky behavior, respondents were less willing to give new hearts to patients with a history of eating a high-fat diet, even less willing to give them to patients with a history of smoking, and the least willing to give them to patients with a history of intravenous drug use.

More surprisingly, respondents were also much less willing to give new hearts to patients with a history of intravenous drug use, even when it was explained to them that such patients have higher survival rates than others after transplantation (ostensibly because of the effects of drug use on the immune system). Most surprisingly, however, there was no relationship at all between the respondents' transplant allocation choices and whether the past behavior of the patients was the cause of heart failure. Even when told that patients with a history of risky behavior were not responsible for their health need (that is, their risky behavior was unrelated to their heart failure), respondents gave them the same low priority as before, in the same order. They did not seem to care at all that in this scenario, the heart failure was entirely a consequence of bad brute luck. It appears that the respondents' judgments did not really reflect beliefs about responsibility. Rather, it seems they reflected disapproval of certain sorts of behavior, regardless of its contribution to health needs.

Initially, luck egalitarianism appears to be able to incorporate individual responsibility into the ethics of health care resource allocation. The way it does it, however, leads to a number of problems. Still, many people argue that responsibility should play a role. So if the implications of luck egalitarianism are unpalatable, the question remains: Is there a better way to take responsibility into account?

6.2 An alternative proposal

Imagine that you are not feeling well, and you worry that you might have a severe illness. So you go to your doctor, and your worry is confirmed. You do have a serious condition. But before your doctor discusses treatment options, he takes out a long questionnaire and starts asking you a series of questions about your lifestyle: Do you, or have you ever smoked? How often do you exercise? What sort of diet do you eat? How many sexual partners have you had recently, and how often do you engage in unsafe sex?

You begin to feel uncomfortable, and not only because of the probing questions. After all, your answers might be medically relevant. But, as your doctor explains, he is not asking them to confirm his diagnosis. Rather, he is asking them to determine the course of treatment that you can get. You see, he explains, treatments are now allocated in a way that takes your responsibility into account. The questionnaire is designed to determine the degree of your responsibility for falling ill. The treatment you are entitled to get depends on your answers. It is possible, if your illness turns out to be your own fault, that you are not offered any treatment at all.

Many people believe that individual responsibility matters. But even they might worry about the way it is taken into account in this example. They might find it intrusive and disrespectful. They might worry that requiring doctors to be the arbitrators of responsibility would lead to a breakdown of trust between doctors and patients, which is the cornerstone of the physician–patient relationship.

Some of those who share these worries have made an alternative proposal for taking responsibility into account. Their basic idea is to account for responsibility in an area other than health care. According to this proposal, smokers and non-smokers should be treated equally at the point of treatment, but, at the same time, a heavy tax should be imposed on tobacco products in order to offset the increased health care costs from tobacco consumption. To return to our earlier example: if Patient A, who has a history of smoking, has also paid a sufficiently high rate of tax on his consumption of tobacco, then it is not justified to give him a lower priority for treatment than to Patient B who does not have a history of smoking. If both of them need a new heart, but there is only one available for transplant, you should flip a coin to decide whether it should go to A or B. At the point of treatment, responsibility has no place. Its proper place is earlier in the course of events.

Of course, tobacco consumption harms not only smokers, but also people who inhale second-hand smoke. Thus, the tax rate must be set at a sufficiently high level to cover the increased health care costs for people whose health is compromised as a result of others' smoking. However, if the tax rate is set sufficiently high, then there is no room for responsibility to affect judgments about health care priorities. This means that the notion of responsibility does not impact decisions regarding the allocation of scarce health care resources.

Note that such policies are actually increasingly popular. Tobacco and alcohol are heavily taxed, although the collected taxes are usually treated as general government revenue, rather than earmarked for the health care system. In response to the growing prevalence of obesity, national and local governments have also experimented with taxes on soft drinks, sweets and unhealthy snacks, and foods with high salt content. For some activities, people are required to have insurance – for instance, for skiing or other dangerous sports. People who have gym memberships might have lower co-payments for certain health care services – which, in effect, raises the contributions of those who do not exercise regularly to the costs of health care. The proposal on the table is that responsibility should be taken into account through policies like these. It contends that people should be held responsible for their *choices*, but not the *consequences* of their choices.

Nevertheless, it is surprisingly difficult to formulate a view that would support this proposal *on the basis of responsibility*. For instance, a simple argument for taxes on the consumption of unhealthy products is that they give people incentives to change their behavior. The taxes hit people where it hurts the most – on their wallets. But this sort of appeal to incentives has nothing to do with responsibility. It gives it no role at all. This does not mean that the incentive-based justification should be rejected. It just means that if what you are after is a justification that rests on responsibility, then the incentive-based justification is not what you are looking for.

Consider another view that has been offered, in different forms, by several philosophers. Their starting point is the claim that there is no substantive difference between the bad effects of option luck and the bad effects of brute luck. Insofar as health outcomes are concerned, every bad health state is a matter of luck, for which nobody should be held responsible. Here is why. Remember that many smokers are lucky enough not to develop heart disease. If these smokers do not develop any serious disease, they manage to dodge a penalty for their irresponsible behavior. But then giving lower priority to the treatment of smokers on the basis of their responsibility merely penalizes unlucky smokers who happen to develop serious diseases. This may be too harsh and unjust towards these unlucky smokers. Thus, even if a person ends up in a bad health state because of his risky behavior, she can be seen as a victim of bad luck for which she should not be held responsible.

Now, if you impose a heavy tax on tobacco products, both lucky and unlucky smokers "pay the price" for their risky behavior. If they pay the price, there is no compelling reason to give lower priority to the treatment of unlucky smokers on the basis of responsibility. Thus, smokers and non-smokers should be treated equally in the allocation of health care resources.

This position can be seen as an extreme version of luck egalitarianism. Every outcome is a matter of luck – they all contain an element of chance. Thus, nobody should be held responsible for the bad effects of their luck, since there is an element of their choices that is out of their control. This view differs from the standard version of luck egalitarianism that we have been discussing in that it takes all luck to involve at least some brute luck. Ultimately, the view does not distinguish between brute and option luck – or at least, it downplays the importance of the distinction.

We call this view *all-luck egalitarianism*. With respect to health care, the interesting difference between standard and all-luck egalitarianism is that standard luck egalitarianism tries to account for responsibility within the health care system, whereas all-luck egalitarianism tries to account for it outside of the health care system, via people's extra contributions to the pool of health care resources.

Although it looks like this sort of view is able to account for the proposal that responsibility for health should be taken into account outside of health care, it is not without its problems. For one thing, traditional luck egalitarians can argue that even if every choice has an element of chance, that surely does not make *all* outcomes beyond your control to the very same degree. Luck egalitarians can concede that, in practice, the distinction between brute luck and option luck is never going to be as clear cut as in theory. But this does not imply that it should not play any role, and thus no one should be held responsible for the bad effects of their luck. There is surely a morally relevant difference between people who occasionally engage in risky behavior and those who are constantly pushing their luck. The all-luck egalitarian position is insensitive to this difference. Accounting for responsibility by taxes on risky activities ignores the differential responsibility of different people. In this way, all-luck egalitarianism is not responsibility-sensitive at all – or at least not responsibility-sensitive enough. So it is unclear that imposing taxes on risky activities and requiring insurance can really be interpreted as holding people responsible, since it ignores differential responsibility.

You might think a policy such as taxing tobacco does take into account differences in responsibility, albeit indirectly. After all, those who smoke more pay more tax. So the policy is sensitive to differences in risky behavior. But not all policies are like this. Even if all motorcyclists are required to purchase insurance, you are unlikely to be able to distinguish between reckless and careful motorcyclists. You have to set the same premiums for all. But if there are many reckless motorcyclists who get into accidents, the premiums are going to have to increase for careful motorcyclists as well. The difference in responsibility between the reckless and the careful motorcyclist is not taken into account. There are many policies that are like this.

Here is another influential view that bears upon this problem. It is called the *fair equality of opportunity view*. It holds that health, and therefore health care, has special, strategic importance for people. Good health is a prerequisite for your pursuing and realizing what you value, and health care protects your ability to pursue and realize what you value. Therefore, health inequalities lead to disadvantage and broader social inequalities; because of this, health inequalities are unfair. The health care system should protect people's fair opportunities in the same way that the prohibition of racial and gender discrimination in hiring and promotion protects everyone's fair opportunities. Thus, every patient should be treated equally. The health care system should not discriminate between them when their health conditions are the same, regardless of their past behavior.

It follows that in the case of the two heart disease patients, A and B should be treated equally. There is no reason to give lower priority to A because he has a history of smoking. The fair equality of opportunity view does not give lower priority to those who engage in risky behaviors. Consequently, there is no place for responsibility in priority setting.

However, the fair equality of opportunity view does not necessarily rule out taxing tobacco, unhealthy food, and similar policies. There is no apparent inconsistency between the fair equality of opportunity view and these policies. Although the view holds that smokers and non-smokers should be treated equally in health care resource allocation, it can take the difference between these two types of patients to be morally relevant outside of the health care system. But, at the same time, it does not explicitly provide a justification for the proposal at all. It does not argue that the proper place for responsibility is in these policies. It does not aim to be a responsibility-sensitive view.

In this section, we have examined the proposal that the proper place for taking responsibility into account is outside of the health care system, rather than at the point of treatment or as part of the allocation of health care resources. The proposal expresses the intuitively attractive idea that people should be held responsible for their choices, but not the consequences of their choices. Traditional luck egalitarianism is unattractive because it introduces responsibility at a point where the consequences of choices have already appeared – when people already suffer the results of their misfortune. In this way, luck egalitarianism is backward-looking: it attributes responsibility at the point of outcomes, and it penalizes only those whose irresponsible behavior has turned out badly.

The proposal we have discussed introduces responsibility at the point of choice. It does not distinguish between those whose irresponsible behavior turns out badly and those who do not suffer any misfortune as the consequence of their choices. In this way, the proposal is not backward-looking. Taxes on alcohol and tobacco or compulsory insurance for risky activities make it unnecessary to consider responsibility within the health care system. Responsibility should not play any role in the allocation of scarce health care resources.

Yet it is not straightforward to provide a responsibility-based justification for the proposal. The fair equality of opportunity view does not consider responsibility for choices. The all-luck egalitarian position, according to its opponents, is not responsibility-sensitive enough. It ignores the differences in responsibility between different people. Of course, perhaps these views could be further developed to provide a justification of the proposal. But even if they are, a more fundamental question remains. Suppose you agree that people should not be held responsible for the consequences of their choices. Should they still be held responsible for their choices? This is the question to which we now turn.

6.3 Are smokers really responsible?

We have presented three views concerning the place of responsibility in health care. The first view, luck egalitarianism, gives responsibility a central role in resource allocation. The two other views, all-luck egalitarianism and the fair equality of opportunity view, do not give responsibility a central role, but they can consistently take it into consideration in other ways. Our initial intuition was that people who engage in risky behaviors, such as smoking, excess consumption of unhealthy food, binge drinking, needle-sharing, dangerous sports, or unprotected casual sex, should be held responsible for their subsequent bad health conditions. Perhaps they should not be held responsible for the consequences of their choices, but they should be held responsible for their choices. So, for instance, they should not get lower priority at the point of care, but they should contribute more to the health care system, through taxes, higher insurance premiums or co-payments, and the like.

However, our initial intuition may be challenged the following way. Perhaps responsibility should not have *any* role in health care. Smokers, binge drinkers, people eating unhealthy diets should not be held responsible for their choices.

If you find this claim too radical, look around. You find very few university professors who smoke cigarettes regularly. Likewise, you find few lawyers, doctors, or high-powered businesspersons who are heavy smokers. These middle-class people are the type you see in gyms, vegetarian restaurants, nice residential areas, and beach resorts. You are far more likely to find smoking and obesity amongst people with lower incomes, lower education, and lower social status. You can easily infer a correlation between unhealthy lifestyle and low socioeconomic status.

This is more than just armchair sociology. A vast body of epidemiological research suggests that there exists a distinct pattern amongst those who engage in risky behavior. Risky behavior, such as smoking or excess drinking, is negatively correlated with income, education, and social status. People with lower socioeconomic status find it more difficult to conform to treatment regimens for diseases such as diabetes and high blood pressure. Thus, income, education, and social status predict the pattern of harmful behavior in the population. From this evidence, it might be tempting to claim that many heavy smokers and binge drinkers did not really choose their lifestyle. Rather, their lifestyles and their risk factors were determined by the circumstances into which they happened to be born. Since they did not have a choice as to which social class they were born into, they are not really responsible for their unhealthy lifestyles. From this, it can be argued that it is unfair to give lower priority to smokers, or to penalize them some other way, on the basis of their potentially harmful and irresponsible lifestyle choices.

There are two conflicting intuitions here. The first is that it is too harsh to place the burden of responsibility onto smokers, drinkers, obese people, and the like. This intuition can be explained in two ways. One way is to emphasize the role that determinism plays in health. People who engage in seemingly irresponsible behavior are not really responsible for their poor health, because they did not truly have free choice in the first place, and therefore could not have behaved otherwise. There is no option luck, and therefore no responsibility whatsoever.

The other way to explain the intuition is to emphasize that people with unhealthy lifestyles are punished too heavily if they are given lower priority in health care resource allocation. It seems that an unduly heavy burden is imposed on them. We call this *triple jeopardy*. The first jeopardy is that these people live in bad socioeconomic circumstances. The second jeopardy is that because of their low socioeconomic status, they are more likely to suffer from bad health conditions. The third jeopardy is that when they are given lower priority, they are punished for their imprudent lifestyle, which they did not choose entirely freely. These poor people – poor in terms of both socio-economic conditions and health status – suffer too much.

The point holds even if responsibility is taken into account indirectly. Consider the idea that people with gym memberships should have lower co-payments for health care services. People of low socioeconomic status are less likely to join gyms or fitness clubs. For one thing, in their social environment, there is less social pressure to do so. In addition, they also have a smaller disposable income and their working and family arrangements are usually less flexible. What the policy ends up doing is to exacerbate their disadvantages by imposing higher co-payments on them.

The second intuition, however, is that there must be some responsibility for irresponsible behavior. Individuals with lower socioeconomic status are not zombies. They have brains, minds, and free will. They may well pick up bad habits as a result of their circumstances. But even if this is true, they still have many chances to overcome their habits and make free and prudent choices. Therefore, these people have genuine free choice, and thus the notion of responsibility can play a significant role in decisions about health care resource allocation.

Now it is clear that the conflict between these two intuitions is closely related to one of the most long-standing philosophical debates – the problem of free will. We will not attempt to discuss this fundamental metaphysical problem here, but merely mention a pragmatic proposal from within the literature on responsibility and distributive justice. This pragmatic theory of responsibility introduces various benchmark levels of responsibility, differentiated by socioeconomic circumstances. Each society lists the factors it wishes to recognize as beyond individual control, and the types of people that display different ranges of behavior. Then, it identifies the median benchmark for each type, and assesses the degree of responsibility on this basis.

For example, plumbers tend to smoke more than schoolteachers. For the sake of simplicity, suppose the median tobacco consumption in the plumber-type is 20 cigarettes each day, whereas the median in the schoolteacher-type is two. Then, if a plumber, Joe, smokes 30 cigarettes each day, he is responsible for the consequences of the ten extra cigarettes he smokes. If he smokes fewer than 20, he is not responsible. On the other hand, if a schoolteacher, James, smokes ten cigarettes a day, he is responsible for the consequences of the eight extra cigarettes he smokes. If he smokes fewer than two, he is not responsible. Thus, this pragmatic theory of responsibility leaves a room for both individual responsibility and for the social determinants of unhealthy behavior. According to this theory, the factors that are beyond your responsibility in the light of your circumstances are morally arbitrary.

A couple of points are worth noting about the pragmatic proposal. First, it is a more complex version of luck egalitarianism. Because of this, it still faces the abandonment objection. Second, as a pragmatic theory of responsibility, it leaves it to society's judgment to decide which factors it wishes to recognize as beyond control and which factors it recognizes as matters of individual responsibility. Recall our earlier worry about this: no one would suggest that women who postpone childbearing should be held responsible for their increased risk of breast cancer. At the same time, respondents of a study were willing to give very low priority to people with a history of intravenous drug use, even when they were told it had nothing to do with these people's health needs. By making attributions of responsibility "pragmatic," there is a danger that this proposal ultimately ends up discriminating between people by the majority's expectations of acceptable behavior.

6.4 The social gradient in health

Once we start taking socioeconomic circumstances into account, we are led to a hotly debated broader issue. This is the issue of the relationship between people's socioeconomic status and their health status.

First of all, it is important to notice that health care is just one of the many factors that contribute to people's health. Other factors such as income, education, sanitation, air quality, housing or workplace safety may be equally, or even more, important. Intuitively, it seems evident that income, which represents economic wealth, is a key contributor to population health. The more affluent people are, the healthier they are. This is indeed true to some extent. Life expectancy tends to be smaller in poor countries and greater in affluent countries. But the truth is a bit more complicated. Here is an example from the 2011 Human Development Report. Table 6.1 shows life expectancy at birth and Gross National Income per capita, measured in terms of constant 2005 purchasing power parity US dollars.

Both Chile and Costa Rica are far poorer than the United States. But life expectancy in these countries is greater than in the US. Actually, Chile is about as rich as Botswana. But its life expectancy is far greater than that of Botswana. Even Costa Rica's life expectancy far exceeds life expectancy in Botswana, while it is poorer. Economic wealth can help build health care infrastructure and improve access to health care. However, the important thing is not economic wealth itself, but the way it is used and distributed in order to improve the factors that influence people's health.

Here is a fact from the vast body of cross-national evidence. Individuals with higher income, greater wealth, higher education, or higher social status live longer and healthier lives. This brute fact persists even in societies where there is equal and universal access to health care. One of the most famous sets of studies demonstrating this relationship is the Whitehall studies. Whitehall is an area of London in which many British civil servants work. The Whitehall studies found a strong correlation between employment grade levels and mortality among civil servants. That is, the rate of disease and mortality increases progressively as grade level goes down. The first Whitehall study (which surveyed 18,000 male civil servants from 1967 onward) reported that men at the bottom of the grade level (for instance, messengers, doorkeepers) faced a risk of

Table 6.1

	Life expectancy at birth (years)	Gross National Income per capita (constant 2005 PPP$)
United States	78.5	43,017
Chile	79.1	13,329
Costa Rica	79.3	10,497
Botswana	53.2	13,049

(Source: UNDP, 2011.)

death four times greater than men at the top of the grade level (administrators). These civil servants all engaged in non-industrial, office-based work. Subsequent studies found a similar gradient in morbidity among women.

As we described earlier, everyone in England has access to health care through the National Health Service. Nonetheless, the Whitehall studies found a striking health gradient in the hierarchy of British civil servants. Workers with lower employment grades were more likely to smoke and therefore to have cardiovascular disease. But even when this risk factor is controlled for, the gradient remains steep. In other words, smokers with lower grade levels were more likely to develop cardiovascular disease than smokers with higher grade levels. Factors such as smoking, high blood pressure, high cholesterol, being overweight, and so on, account for only some of the gradient in mortality. This means that they cannot explain all of the observed differences. Workers at lower grade levels have worst health outcomes even when the effect of all the other factors are set aside. If this finding can be generalized, it suggests that people with lower socioeconomic status face higher mortality and morbidity risks even if all other factors – including lifestyle choices – are set aside.

Britain is widely known for being a class-stratified society. But a similar relationship between socioeconomic status and the health gradient is found in other countries. In the United States, the life expectancy at birth of the least educated white men is 67.5 years; for those who have a college or higher degree, it is 80.4. That is an enormous gap. But racial inequalities in mortality are even more pronounced. The life expectancy gap between Asian American males and high-risk urban African American males is 15.4 years; in the case of women, the gap between Asian females and low-income rural African American women in the South is 12.8 years. African American infant mortality rates are two times higher than infant mortality rates for white Americans.

There is a strong correlation between inequalities in health and inequalities in socioeconomic status. This fact is not surprising once you recognize that socioeconomic conditions affect people's health, and the unequal distribution of socioeconomic conditions predict the unequal distribution of morbidity and mortality. To be sure, health care affects people's health-related quality of life, but it is just one of many factors. Some of the factors are not clinical, but they are closely related to health (vaccination, sanitation, nutrition, stress). Other factors are more general and further removed from health care (education, income, housing, workplace safety). All of these factors jointly determine people's health-related quality of life. When these determinants are distributed unequally, it is not surprising that corresponding inequalities in health appear.

Here is an interesting question to ask. Does the social gradient in health give rise to an ethical concern? Some people might say that as long as equal access to health care is secured, there is no reason to care about the health gradient. Call this the *equal access view*. Proponents of this view would claim that a health care system should ensure equal access to health care to everyone in a given society, and that anything further is beyond ethical or governmental concern (at least as far as health is concerned). They might also add that health inequalities are not a matter of social responsibility, but rather a matter for individual responsibility. At first glance, this view might look attractive. But it is unclear whether it continues to be plausible in light of what is now known about the correlation between health and socioeconomic inequalities.

As a matter of fact, governments and international organizations care about health inequalities beyond ensuring equal access. Why? As far as we can see, there are two reasons. They can be explained by the two views we examined in Section 6.2: the fair equality of opportunity view and all-luck egalitarianism.

The fair equality of opportunity view offers the first type of reason. According to this view, health equality itself is desirable. Health is special in the sense that it protects each person's opportunities, no matter what she wants to achieve in the course of her life. Society should ensure that the playing field is equal for everyone to go about pursuing their life plan. Therefore, health equality itself is desirable and required by justice. It is not possible, however, to directly redistribute health – it cannot be transferred from one person to the next in order to equalize it. Nevertheless, the socially controllable determinants of health (such as income, wealth, opportunities for education and employment) can be redistributed. In order to promote health equality, the fair equality of opportunity view claims, it is desirable to aim for more equality in socioeconomic conditions.

The second reason is given by all-luck egalitarianism. All-luck egalitarians would claim that health inequality is a result of differences in luck for which nobody should be held responsible. People do not choose to be born into the lower ranks of society, and they should not be held responsible for having a lower socioeconomic status. Therefore, people should not be held responsible for the resulting health inequalities. From this, all-luck egalitarians would conclude that you should neutralize the effects of brute luck in health by neutralizing the effects of brute luck in socioeconomic conditions. More specifically, they would claim that you should aim for more equality in socioeconomic conditions, which would subsequently result in more equality in people's health outcomes. These two views provide reasons in support of aiming for health equality via the redistribution of socioeconomic conditions.

6.5 Social justice and health care rationing

Some countries take seriously the gradient in morbidity and mortality due to the social determinants of health and have made attempts to reduce it by introducing policies that aim at more equality in socio-economic conditions. For example, during Tony Blair's Labour government, Britain's Acheson Report recommended a set of health policies that addressed health inequalities through "upstream" or broader social policies.[1] The Commission on Social Determinants of Health of the World Health Organization made similar proposals.

The implicit belief behind this trend is that the reduction of inequalities in socioeconomic conditions will subsequently reduce health inequalities. That is, if you distribute the socially controllable determinants of health more equally, then you can subsequently reduce health inequalities. This idea takes the correlation between the two types of inequalities to be a *causal* relation. That is, socioeconomic inequality causes health inequality, and therefore the reduction of socioeconomic inequalities is expected to reduce health inequalities. But strictly speaking, this idea does not follow from the fact that there is a *correlation* between the two types of inequalities. The correlation merely implies that inequalities in socioeconomic conditions *predict* inequalities in morbidity and mortality. As the familiar slogan says, correlation does not imply causation.

Consider two cases. First, intravenous drug users tend to be poor in terms of both socioeconomic circumstances and health. But it is not the case that their poor health is caused by their poor socioeconomic circumstances. Rather, their poor health is caused by their drug addiction. Although there is a correlation between poor health and poor socioeconomic circumstances, the cause is drug addiction, not socioeconomic circumstances. Of course, it could be claimed that bad socioeconomic circumstances tend to cause drug addiction, and that drug addiction in turn causes poor health. Hence, the ultimate cause is bad socioeconomic circumstances. In practice, it is very difficult to identify the ultimate causes of poor health.

Second, even though there might be many cases where you can actually identify the causal chain from poor socioeconomic circumstances to poor health, you can easily find examples where the causal relation goes in the opposite direction. On the one hand, some people retire early because they are too ill or disabled to continue working. These people tend to have limited income while having large medical bills every month. Poor health conditions can cause economic hardship. On the other hand, healthier people can continue to work and they are thus socioeconomically better off even in their old age. In such cases, health inequality causes socioeconomic inequality. Thus, you must be careful when you try to infer a moral judgment from the correlation between the two types of inequalities. The correlation may work both ways.

There is some research according to which one major causal factor is level of education. Intuitively, it is not difficult to see why: people with higher levels of education tend to earn more and stay healthier. So if you provide better opportunities for education to those who come from less advantaged backgrounds, you can expect health and socioeconomic inequalities to be reduced. This is just one possible way to go about reducing inequalities, but it is not the only way.

Nonetheless, at this point, you might be led back to the idea of a robust causal relation from socioeconomic circumstances to health. It might be argued that it is people from families with higher incomes and higher social status who are more likely to attain a higher level of education. The top universities across the world are typically upper-middle-class universities. Thus, you might be led back to the claim that the *cause of the cause* of health inequalities is income and wealth – and therefore what you should aim to equalize is income and wealth. Although it is simple enough to acknowledge that there is a social gradient in morbidity and mortality, there is no simple solution as to what should be redistributed in order to mitigate it.

We have seen that there are difficulties with understanding the correlation between inequalities in socioeconomic conditions and inequalities in health. Because of these difficulties, it is not clear what ethical conclusions should be drawn from them. But one conclusion seems clear enough: if you are concerned with health inequalities that exist in a population, it is very unlikely that you can address them within the health care system only. The same holds if your concern is not with health inequalities directly, but with improving health outcomes for the worse off social groups. Redistributing health care resources to reduce health inequalities can only take you so far. You need broader social policy to achieve your goal.

Where does that leave us? We began this chapter by noting that our discussion so far has focused on health-related factors only: health-related quality of life, the cost-effectiveness of interventions, the problem of aggregating health benefits, and so on. In this "health-only" framework, ethical questions about the allocation of health care resources are settled by focusing on health benefits, mostly ignoring other characteristics of the population, including the patterns of social and economic conditions within it. (We say "mostly," since we introduced some considerations that were not directly related to health in Section 4.5.) We argued that the health-only framework has intuitive appeal: when scarce health care resources must be rationed, your concern should be with health.

This chapter considered two challenges to this idea. The first focused on individual responsibility for health. Initially, it seems that it would be unjust not to take into account people's responsibility for their health conditions when scarce resources are allocated. This idea is supported by luck egalitarianism, perhaps the currently most influential theory of distributive justice. Its application to health gives a central role to individual responsibility.

Nevertheless, we have argued that there are many problems with the way luck egalitarianism accounts for responsibility in health care. These problems provide a good illustration of the more general difficulties for the theory. We have concluded that luck egalitarianism should not be accepted in health care, and responsibility should not have the sort of role that it envisages.

There is, however, another way responsibility for health can be taken into account. It is to do it outside of the health care system, through policies that make people take responsibility for their choices, but not the consequences of their choices. We objected that such policies are difficult to justify on the basis of responsibility. To be sure, they are compatible with some views on distributive justice in health care, but they are not, strictly speaking, entailed by them. Consequently, it is difficult to justify any role for individual responsibility in health care. Perhaps except for marginal cases, it is not a relevant factor in health care resource allocation. It is not an ethical concern in this area.

No doubt some readers will remain unpersuaded. They might think it is difficult to accept a conclusion that conflicts with a moral intuition that they share with many others. Indeed, a common presumption in discussions of responsibility for health is that almost everyone believes that responsibility should be an object of moral concern. But it is interesting to note that this, in fact, is far from the case – at least on the basis of what we know from empirical studies on people's moral beliefs about this issue. It is true that in most studies in which respondents are asked to set priorities among different patients, many of them do take into account the patients' history of risky behavior and their responsibility for their health need. But it is usually only around half, and often even below that, of the respondents who do that. What this shows is that people are sharply divided on the issue of responsibility. For many of them, it is evident that it should play a role in health care resource allocation; for many, it is equally evident that it should not.

It is important to note that people in the latter group do not need to oppose policies such as taxing tobacco or unhealthy foods or requiring extra insurance from those who engage in dangerous sports. They can justify them on the basis of incentives: they can agree that it is

permissible to prohibit or discourage risky behavior and encourage prudent behavior.

The second challenge to the health-only framework comes from the
growing body of evidence on the social determinants of health. Noting
the close relationship between health outcomes and social and economic
factors, some people might argue that the health-only framework is too
narrow: the ethics of the allocation of health care resources must be part
of a broader theory of social justice. It is unfruitful to discuss it separately.
In particular, when scarce health care resources must be rationed, choices
must be made on the basis of that broader theory. Hence most of our
discussion in this book is too narrow.

There are two ways to understand this challenge. On the one hand, the
claim might be that the allocation of health care resources should focus on
reducing disadvantage in general – instead of narrowly focusing on, for
instance, selecting interventions that are the best value for money or making
trade-offs between aggregate health benefits and the benefits of the worst off.

But the health-only framework, as we have seen, is not incompatible
with additional moral considerations. It does not have to take a narrow
approach in which only cost-effectiveness matters. In addition, the challenge
ignores the lessons from the evidence on the social determinants of health.
Because health is affected by so many other factors, health care is probably
not be the best area to address broader disadvantages. If unjust social and
economic conditions prevail in society, there is relatively little that health
care can do to reduce disadvantage, because those conditions are likely to
maintain and reproduce inequalities in health, despite your best efforts.

On the other hand, the challenge can be interpreted in a different way.
It might claim that the health-only framework is too narrow, since the
best way to address ethical concerns in the allocation of health care
resources is through the socially controllable determinants of health.
Rather than trying to work out ethical principles for priority setting in
health care, you should focus on a more just and equal distribution of the
social determinants of health – income, education, housing, and so on. By
addressing these determinants, you can reduce inequalities in health and
promote population health.

The problem with this understanding of the challenge is that it ignores
the fact of scarcity in health care. Even if other social and economic conditions are improved for all, the need for allocating health care resources
remains. Rationing decisions still have to be made. Even the most equal
and developed societies need to make sure that the available resources are
allocated fairly and efficiently within health care. Their allocation raises
its own ethical issues. It needs its own ethical principles. We have argued
that the best way to address the ethical issues in health care rationing is
to remain in the health-only framework.

Chapter summary

Luck egalitarianism aims to take into account people's responsibility for the consequences of their choices. On this view, health inequalities are not unjust if they are a result of people's free choices. Luck egalitarianism captures the importance of individual responsibility for health care rationing very well. However, it runs into two problems. One is the abandonment objection. The other is that the scope of responsibility for health outcomes may be limited because socioeconomic status, which few people intentionally choose, affects lifestyle and therefore health outcomes. There is also difficulty for views that aim to hold people responsible for their choices, rather than the consequences of their choices. We have argued that responsibility for health outcomes should not be a factor in the allocation of health care resources.

Without doubt, the social gradient in health gives rise to an ethical concern. It may be claimed that priorities in health care should be set with a view to reducing this gradient. It may also be claimed that the allocation of health care resources should be determined by some broader theory of social justice. We have rejected both of these claims. The allocation of health care resources and the social gradient in health should be treated as separate ethical issues.

Discussion questions

1. Should health care systems pay for the costs of bariatric surgery (a procedure to reduce the size of the stomach with a gastric band) for people whose unhealthy diet has contributed to their obesity? Or should these people be expected to reduce the risks associated with obesity by adopting healthy lifestyles?
2. "I am a heavy smoker. But I am also from a disadvantaged socio-economic class, and all my friends and neighbors smoke a lot. Therefore, I cannot be held responsible for my smoking habit and possible lung cancer. If our health care system gives priority to non-smokers, that is unjust." What do you think about this argument?
3. Some people argue that incentives for healthier choices (for instance, taxes on sugary beverages and foods with trans fats) are unjustifiably intrusive and overly paternalistic. Where should the line be drawn between health promotion and respect for individual choices?
4. In order to reduce the social gradient of health, people with lower socioeconomic status may need *better* access to health care. Should they be offered better access even if this undermines *equal* access to everyone?
5. In 2008, the Commission on Social Determinants of Health of the World Health Organization published its final report, *Closing the Gap*

in a Generation. The Commission argued that "reducing health inequalities is, for the Commission on Social Determinants of Health, an ethical imperative. Social injustice is killing people on a grand scale" (CSDH 2008). Do you agree with the Commission's assessment?

Further readings

Wikler (2004) offers a good general overview of personal and social responsibility for health. (We also borrowed the breast cancer example in Section 6.1 from him.) Segall (2010) is the most comprehensive work on luck egalitarianism in health and health care. Cappelen and Norheim (2005), in contrast, argue that people should be held responsible for their choices, rather than the consequences of their choices, in health care. See also Wilkinson (1999). The research about heart transplants for people with a history of smoking, intravenous drug use, and high-fat diet is reported in Ubel *et al.* (1999). Olsen *et al.* (2003) gives an overview of empirical research on people's views about responsibility in health care resource allocation. The pragmatic theory of responsibility is proposed by Roemer (1993); a version of prioritarianism that incorporates responsibility is defended by Arneson (2000). The large literature on the social gradient of health starts with the Whitehall studies of Marmot *et al.* (1984). Marmot (2004) is an excellent introduction to the topic. For US data, see Murray *et al.* (2006). Daniels (2008) offers a clear explanation of how and why the social gradient of health is an important issue for ethics. Deaton (2002) raises powerful objections to arguments that more equal socioeconomic status will bring about more equal health outcomes. Many of the issues in this chapter are discussed in more detail in the contributions to Eyal *et al.* (2013).

Note

1 Available at http://www.archive.official-documents.co.uk/document/doh/ih/ih.htm.

Conclusion

Health care rationing is the controlled allocation of health care resources. Many people are uncomfortable with, or downright hostile to, the idea of rationing health care. So it is worth asking what would happen if there was no control at all in the allocation of health care resources.

The answer is that some sort of rationing would still take place. Whether or not anyone attempts to control the allocation of health care resources, the problem of scarcity remains. It still needs to be faced. Who would ultimately decide how health care resources are used? The answer is obvious enough. It would be frontline health care workers – doctors, nurses, general practitioners – as well as the managers and administrators of clinics, hospitals, and general practices.

If there is no attempt to control the allocation of health care resources, then frontline health care workers must do it at their own judgment, without general guidelines. They have to manage the scarcity, because no one else does. It hardly needs spelling out why this would be undesirable. For one thing, it would be unfair. It may well be the case, for instance, that patients in one hospital would be able to receive a certain treatment that patients in other hospitals could not. Frontline rationing is also unlikely to be transparent. It would be difficult to keep track of what decisions are made and why. In the absence of general policies, it would be impossible, for instance, for patients to compare the practices at one hospital to the practices at another. More importantly, if rationing took place at the bedside, it would often be arbitrary. Physicians and hospitals would have to make their own judgments about the allocation of resources. There are no safeguards that those judgments would be rational and morally justifiable. Unprincipled bedside rationing raises the risks of unintentional mistakes, prejudice, and corruption.

Ironically, what the opponents of the rationing of health care resources are often the most worried about is bedside rationing. They find it unacceptable that doctors should ever put limits on the care that they offer to their patients. What these opponents do not realize is that the refusal to allocate health care resources along general moral principles, and in a way that applies across the whole range of health care institutions, would lead to precisely the sort of unfair, unaccountable, and arbitrary choices in health care that they most want to avoid.

It is sometimes said that doctors, nurses, and other frontline health care workers should not be forced to limit the care that they offer to patients. They should not have to think about scarcity. It would be an unduly heavy burden on them to have to make rationing decisions. But if there is no control on the allocation of resources, this is precisely what they are forced to do. Health care should be rationed, so that it does not have to be rationed at the bedside. Of course, it might still be necessary for frontline health care workers to limit care. But if health care resources are allocated on the basis of clear moral principles, frontline health care workers have to make difficult decisions less often – and when they do, they can make them fairly, transparently, and accountably.

Leaving rationing decisions for the bedside is a bad idea also because it actually increases scarcity. Worldwide, it is estimated, 20–40 percent of health care spending is wasted. For the United States, the estimates are around 30 percent. As the 2010 World Health Report put it, "health-care systems haemorrhage money" (WHO 2010). Probably not all of the loss can be attributed to the inefficient use of services. A lot of waste results from lack of coordination within the health care system. But at least some of the waste is from ignoring the cost-effectiveness of interventions, unnecessary diagnostic and testing procedures, unnecessary referrals to specialists, the overprescription of pharmaceuticals, and the like.

All of these problems show the need for the general rationing of health care along clear and justified moral principles. As opposed to the alternatives, the general rationing of health care can be fair, accountable, and transparent. Health care rationing is not only inevitable, but it is morally desirable. It is in the interest of all of us.

Of course, many goods are scarce. Yet most people do not worry about their allocation. Most people do not worry that not everyone can afford Caribbean holidays. There is a limited supply of Caribbean holidays, but the market ensures that they are allocated efficiently. They are allocated to those who are willing and able to pay for them. It is true that not everyone will have access to them; but for most people, this is not a matter of justice.

But health is a peculiar sort of good. Most people not only do not know the value of different interventions and services, they do not even know which ones they need. Health care workers do not merely provide services to people – they help them determine what services they need to begin with. This is only one reason health care is unlike the market for Caribbean holidays. Yet, even if you ignore this, an even more important difference remains: health is a matter of ethical concern in the way Caribbean holidays are not. Health is one of the most important components of well-being. In its absence, it is difficult to pursue your plans, to realize what you value, and generally to enjoy life.

We have argued that the rationing of health care is in everyone's interest: it benefits all of us. But we have also argued that this is true only if rationing is based on justified, general ethical principles. It is a task for ethical theory to formulate those principles.

But you may wonder why it should not be left to the judgment of the people. Why should the principles for the allocation of health care resources need ethical justification? After all, other justifications are also available. For instance, the principles could be justified on the basis of a democratic process. Rationing affects everyone. So citizens should decide on the principles that should govern it. There are democratic procedures that can be used for these decisions. People should have a voice, either directly or through their elected representatives, in formulating principles for health care resource allocation.

But moral justification is not a majoritarian procedure. Moral questions cannot be decided by taking votes. Neither can they be decided by politicians only. Politicians are notoriously vulnerable to pressures by their electorate, their prospects for reelection, and powerful interest groups like medical associations, the pharmaceutical industry, patient groups of certain types, and so on. There are good reasons to delegate rationing decisions to agencies and bodies that are more removed from these immediate pressures, like NICE is in England and Wales and PHARMAC is in New Zealand.

Of course, health care resource allocation choices are already left to citizens and their elected representatives. Philosophers do not, and cannot, make these decisions for them. The most philosophers can do is to make their arguments, hoping that they will convince others and influence the democratic process. What they can offer is their expertise in formulating ethical principles and evaluating moral arguments.

None of this is to say that the rationing of health care must be unrelated to people's views. Rationing choices must be *legitimate*: acceptable to those who will have to live with their consequences, even when they are disadvantaged by them. Fairness, accountability, and transparency are all part of legitimacy. Rationing choices need ethical justification if they are to be legitimate in the eyes of the population.

How real-life rationing choices can be made in ways that increase or maintain their legitimacy is one of the most pressing practical issues for health care systems worldwide. It is also one of the philosophically most challenging – and one that we had to set aside in this book. Our focus has been narrower. Whatever else may contribute to the legitimacy of health care resource allocation choices, efficiency and fairness, two ethical ideals that we have discussed extensively, will have important roles.

At the beginning of the book, we identified two central ideas for the ethics of health care rationing: fairness and benefit maximization. We have argued that benefit maximization requires the measurement of health benefits (for instance, by QALYs) and the use of cost-effectiveness analysis to identify the most efficient ways to allocate resources. We noted that fairness and benefit maximization can conflict, and argued that it is useful to think of fairness as a constraint on the maximization of benefits. We went on to identify the contexts in which such a constraint seems desirable.

We have seen many examples. There was the question whether the use of cost-effectiveness analysis *unfairly* discriminates against people with disabilities. Or whether the prohibition of topping up in the NHS is *unfair* towards those who can pay for expensive medicines out-of-pocket without burdening the health care system. Or whether those who have had a full life should have diminished claims on social resources so that everyone can have a *fair* go at a full life. In the rescue case, our question was whether it is *fair* to give each person the same chance of being saved. And we asked whether inequalities in health are *unfair*, especially given what we know about their correlation with other sorts of inequalities and disadvantage. The list is not exhaustive. There are other contexts within health care – many of which we could not discuss here – in which the problem of fairness arises.

Why didn't we start our analysis with offering an account of fairness, given the central role it plays in the ethics of health care rationing? It is because, surprisingly, there is no generally accepted account of fairness in ethics. In fact, there isn't even a generally accepted definition of the concept. Indeed, some philosophers will even object to the way we have used the word! Given such disagreements, it is more useful to discover what fairness demands in different contexts, rather than start out with an account of fairness and use it to answer every question. It is unlikely that anyone would be convinced if we followed that route. Instead, we offered what seems to us a plausible, broad definition – fairness as a constraint on benefit maximization – and tried to see how far it takes us by considering different problems.

Yet here, at the end, we are still not in a position to offer a full account of fairness – or even an account of fairness in health care. But this is not a failure. For one thing, population-level bioethics, the branch of philosophy that addresses the issues of health care rationing, is a very new field. We have only been able to take some initial steps in this book. But, at the same time, our analysis has had some important results. We have argued that costs and benefits are relevant moral considerations in the allocation of health care resources. We have defended cost-effectiveness analysis from the disability discrimination objection. We have suggested that equity weights can help incorporate some moral considerations into priority setting. We have suggested that if age is morally relevant, then prioritarian age-weighting is the most acceptable way to take it into account.

Importantly, we have defended the aggregation thesis – the idea that benefits to different people can be added up and compared across different groups. We suggested that an aggregative view, prioritarianism, can address some of the worries that opponents of aggregation have. Finally, we argued that responsibility should not have a central role in health care and defended the ethics of health care rationing from those who would subsume it under broader theories of justice.

Let us close this book with two remarks to put our analysis into perspective.

The first remark concerns the scope of our analysis. It is important to recognize what we have *not* claimed in the course of our argument. We made no claims about institutional matters such as the way a health care system should be organized or the way it should be financed. As we explained early on, our argument is not affected by whether health care is provided through private insurance sold by companies in a market-based system, or provided publicly from general tax revenues or through social insurance. In all cases, health care rationing does inevitably occur – if not by the government, then by insurance providers. It is just as important that it is done fairly, accountably, and transparently when it is done by private industry.

It is also worth emphasizing some of the things that are *not* entailed by the arguments in this book. Although we have emphasized the importance of the scarcity of health care resources, it does not follow that the only way to deal with it is to limit health care or access to health care. We would be upset if our analysis in this book was misrepresented by those who want to cut health care expenditures. There is nothing in our argument that suggests that health care expenditures should be shrunk or the size of government should be reduced. Our analysis is logically independent of the size of health care budgets. In addition, the case for rationing is not a case for the centralization of health care systems. We had nothing to say on how, where, and by whom health care services should be delivered, whether health care institutions should be privately or publicly owned, or at what level decisions about health care resource uses should be made.

The second remark is that our analysis has taken it for granted that nobody should be excluded from general access to health care. There is no compelling reason to manage scarcity of resources by denying access to health care for some part of the population. We do not know of anyone who would make this argument. A rationing scheme that would provide access to some people at the expense of denying access to others fails to pass a basic moral test.

The task that is now faced by health care systems all around the world is to provide equal access to health care to everyone in the face of increasing scarcity. In the next few decades, scarcity in health care is certain to increase. This is partly driven by technology and the benefit expansion that accompanies the introduction of new procedures, interventions, and services. But it is also driven by demographic change: many countries, especially in the developed world, are aging rapidly. In countries that belong to the OECD, currently around 14 percent of the population is over 65. By 2050, the ratio of those who are over 65 is expected to double, to close to a third of the population. This will have a profound influence on the health care sector.

Moreover, it is not only that more people will survive to old age: those who do will also live longer. Currently, in OECD countries, 65-year-old women can expect, on average, to live another 19.9 years and men can expect to live another 16.4 years. By 2050, life expectancy at 65 for women is forecast to increase to 23.5 years, and for men 19.5 years. In these countries, health care spending on those who are over 65 already accounts for 40–50 percent of health care expenditures; their per capita health care costs are three to five times higher than the share of those who are in other age groups.

In affluent countries, health care spending has grown faster than GDP for several decades, and the difference is expected to increase in the future. Even if current levels of spending on health care are maintained or increased, it is highly likely that the spending is not going to be able to keep pace with increasing health care needs. Choices about the rationing of health care will become more and more pressing and difficult in the future.

Low- and middle-income countries face even more daunting challenges. As they are developing, they have to broaden access to health care while ensuring that their health care systems remain affordable. Many of the poorest countries still struggle with the tragic consequences of lack of basic health care. They have to make difficult choices every day. For poor and affluent countries alike, the allocation of health care resources will become one of the greatest moral challenges.

This book provides only starting points for thinking through these issues. We have introduced many concepts, discussed many arguments, endorsed certain positions and rejected others, but mostly have just raised a lot of difficult questions. Our purpose has been to introduce you to this area and provide you with the equipment to think about these questions further on your own and together with others in your community. If there is one thing we would like our readers to take away from this book, it is the recognition of the importance of philosophical thinking in practical contexts. When you are presented with an argument, you should always ask what that argument implies and how far it can take you. Even a good argument might have unpalatable implications that can be discovered only through careful reasoning and analysis. If the implication is unpalatable, you may have to go back and revise the original argument. To revise the argument, you have to decide which part of it you should modify. This sort of back-and-forth is essentially philosophical – Socrates invented it more than two thousand years ago. Many practical issues, but especially the allocation of health care resources, require this sort of philosophical thinking. Ultimately, our aim has been to compel our readers to think about difficult real-life issues philosophically.

Glossary

Age-weighting   The idea that health benefits have different value depending on the age of the beneficiary.

Aggregation problem   The debate concerning whether small benefits for a large number of people can morally outweigh large losses for a small number of people.

Aggregation thesis   The proposition that benefits to different people can be added up and compared across different groups for moral evaluation. A direct implication of the thesis is that small benefits for a large number of people can morally outweigh large losses for a small number of people.

Consequentialism   The moral view that the rightness of an act is determined solely by the goodness of its consequences. See deontology.

Cost-effectiveness analysis (CEA)   A tool for evaluating the overall health benefits of interventions and health care services, comparing the ratios of their costs and benefits.

Deontology (deontological theory)   The moral view that the rightness or wrongness of an act can be determined independently of the value of its consequences. See consequentialism.

Disability discrimination objection   An objection to the use of cost-effectiveness analysis according to which it disadvantages people with disabilities or chronic health conditions in the allocation of health care resources.

Disability weights   The quality-adjustment factors used in disability-adjusted life years (DALYs).

Disability-adjusted life year (DALY)   A measure of disease burden expressed as the sum of the number of years of life lost due to disability and the number of years of life lived with disability.

Egalitarianism   The view that it is in itself bad if some people are worse off than others, regardless of how the inequality is brought about. See luck egalitarianism.

EQ-5D   A standardized survey method for use as a generic measure of health-related quality of life. Its dimensions are: (1) mobility,

(2) self-care, (3) usual activities, (4) pain/discomfort, and (5) anxiety/depression.

Equal access view   The view that everyone should have equal access to health care, but not necessarily to equal health status.

Equity weighting   The idea that health benefits have different value depending on how bad the health states of patients are. In particular, health benefits to those whose health states are worse have greater weight. See prioritarianism.

Fair chances   The view that people are entitled to a chance of receiving a scarce good, where the chance is proportional to the strength of their claim to that good.

Fair equality of opportunity view   The view that health has a special role to protect people's opportunity and therefore health policy should be designed in order to secure reasonable equality of their opportunity.

Fair innings argument   The argument that people who have already had sufficient time to carry out their life plans should have weaker claims on social resources, including health care, than younger people who have not had a similar amount of time.

Health-adjusted life expectancy (HALE)   The number of years a person can expect to live from some point in her life (e.g. birth), weighed by some adjustment factor for health-related quality of life for those years.

Leveling down objection   An objection to egalitarianism according to which it is absurd that egalitarianism judges that it is, at least in one respect, better if a better off person is made worse off for the sake of greater equality while no one else is made better off.

Leximin (the lexicographic extension of maximin)   The non-aggregative principle according to which the best outcome is that which maximizes the well-being of the worst off; or that which maximizes the well-being of the second worst off if the levels of the well-being of the worst off are the same in all outcomes; or that which maximizes the well-being of the third worst off if the levels of well-being of the worst off and the second worst off are the same in all outcomes; and so on.

Luck egalitarianism   The view that it is bad if some people are worse off than others through no fault or choice of their own. See egalitarianism.

Maximin   The principle that the best outcome is the one that maximizes the well-being of the worst off.

Number problem   The problem concerning how the case for saving the greater number of individuals can be morally justified without adding up the good of lives saved (i.e. without appealing to the aggregation thesis).

Principle of pairwise comparison   The non-aggregative principle that chooses the outcome in which the maximum loss is minimized from individual standpoints.

Prioritarianism   The view that the right action is that which maximizes the sum of weighted well-being where the weights are determined by an increasing, strictly concave function. That is, a unit of benefit has greater weight the worse off the beneficiary is. It is a consequentialist view.

Pure time preference   The disposition to give greater weight to present benefits than future benefits.

Quality-adjusted life year (QALY)   A measure of the value of health outcomes that combines the health-related quality of life associated with a health outcome and the time during which a person lives with that health outcome.

Rating scale   A method for eliciting health state evaluations in which respondents indicate the value of health states on a numerical scale.

Social determinants of health   Social and economic conditions that affect health outcomes, and the distribution of health outcomes, in a population.

Social gradient in health   Inequalities in health outcomes between different socioeconomic groups within the population.

Standard gamble   A method for eliciting health state evaluations in which respondents have to make trade-offs between living with a health outcome on the one hand, and a treatment gamble in which they can be restored to full health with probability p or die with probability $(1 - p)$. The value of a health state is determined by the value of p at which respondents are indifferent between living with the health state and the treatment gamble.

Time trade-off   A method for eliciting health state evaluations in which respondents have to make trade-offs between living with a health outcome for some time and living in full health for a shorter period of time. The value of a health state is determined by the amount of time respondents are willing to sacrifice to avoid the health state.

Triage   The procedure for determining the priority of treatments based on the severity of the condition of patients used in medical emergencies. Patients for whom immediate treatment can make a difference between life and death are given priority compared to those who are likely to survive without immediate treatment and those who are likely to die even with immediate treatment.

Utilitarianism   The view according to which an act is right if and only if it maximizes the sum of people's well-being. It is a consequentialist view.

Bibliography

Alexander, Shana. (1962) "They Decide Who Lives, Who Dies, Medical Miracle and a Moral Burden of a Small Committee." *LIFE Magazine*, November, 102–27.

Anand, Sudhir, Fabienne Peter and Amartya Sen, eds. (2004) *Public Health, Ethics, and Equity*. Oxford: Oxford University Press.

Arneson, Richard J. (2000) "Luck Egalitarianism and Prioritarianism." *Ethics* 110(2), 339–49.

Bell, J. M. and Susan Mendus, eds. (1988) *Philosophy and Medical Welfare*. Cambridge: Cambridge University Press.

Blumstein, James F. (1997) "The Oregon Experiment: The Role of Cost-Benefit Analysis in the Allocation of Medicaid Funds." *Social Science and Medicine* 45 (4), 545–54.

Bognar, Greg. (2008a) "Age-Weighting." *Economics and Philosophy* 24(2), 167–89.

——(2008b) "Well-Being and Health." *Health Care Analysis* 16(2), 97–113.

——(2010) "Does Cost Effectiveness Analysis Unfairly Discriminate against People with Disabilities?" *Journal of Applied Philosophy* 27(4), 394–408.

——(2011) "Impartiality and Disability Discrimination." *Kennedy Institute of Ethics Journal* 21(1), 1–23.

Brock, Dan W. (1988) "Ethical Issues in Recipient Selection for Organ Transplantation." In Deborah Mathieu (ed.) *Organ Substitution Technology: Ethical, Legal and Public Policy Issues*, 86–99. Boulder, CO: Westview Press.

——(1993) "Quality of Life Measures in Health Care and Medical Ethics." In Martha Nussbaum and Amartya Sen (eds.) *The Quality of Life*, 95–132. Oxford: Clarendon Press.

——(2002a) "The Separability of Health and Well-Being." In Murray *et al.* (2002), 115–20.

——(2002b) "Priority to the Worse Off in Health-Care Resource Prioritization." In Rosamond Rhodes, Margaret P. Battin, and Anita Silvers (eds.) *Medicine and Social Justice: Essays on the Distribution of Health Care*, 362–72. New York: Oxford University Press.

——(2004) "Ethical Issues in the Use of Cost-Effectiveness Analysis for the Prioritization of Health Care Resources." In Anand *et al.* (2004), 201–23.

——(2009) "Cost-Effectiveness and Disability Discrimination." *Economics and Philosophy* 25(1), 27–47.

Broome, John. (1988) "Good, Fairness and QALYs." In Bell and Mendus (1988), 57–73.

——(1994) "Discounting the Future." *Philosophy and Public Affairs* 23(2), 128–56. Reprinted in Broome (1999*a*).

——(1999*a*) *Ethics Out of Economics*. Cambridge: Cambridge University Press.

——(1999*b*) "Qalys." In Broome (1999*a*), 196–213.

——(2002) "Measuring the Burden of Disease by Aggregating Well-Being." In Murray *et al.* (2002), 91–113.

Cappelen, Alexander W. and Ole F. Norheim. (2005) "Responsibility in Health Care: A Liberal Egalitarian Approach." *Journal of Medical Ethics* 31(8), 476–80.

CSDH. (2008) *Closing the Gap in a Generation: Health Equity through Action on the Social Determinants of Health. Final Report of the Commission on Social Determinants of Health.* Geneva: World Health Organization. Available at http://www.who.int/social_determinants/thecommission/finalreport/en/index.html.

Daniels, Norman. (2008) *Just Health: Meeting Health Needs Fairly*. Cambridge: Cambridge University Press.

Daniels, Norman, Frances M. Kamm, Eric Rakowski, John Broome, and Mary Ann Baily. (1994) "Meeting the Challenges of Justice & Rationing." *Hastings Center Report* 24(4), 27–42.

Deaton, Angus. (2002) "Policy Implications of the Gradient of Health and Wealth." *Health Affairs* 21(2), 13–30.

Driver, Julia. (2007) *Ethics: The Fundamentals*. Malden, MA: Blackwell.

Eddy, David M. (1992) "Cost-Effectiveness Analysis: A Conversation with My Father." *JAMA* 267(12), 1669–75.

Eyal, Nir, Samia A. Hurst, Ole F. Norheim, and Dan Wikler, eds. (2013) *Inequalities in Health: Concepts, Measures, and Ethics*. New York: Oxford University Press.

Fenton, Elizabeth. (2010) "Making Fair Funding Decisions for High Cost Cancer Care: The Case of Herceptin in New Zealand." *Public Health Ethics* 3(2), 137–46.

Froberg, Debra G. and Robert L. Kane. (1989*a*) "Methodology for Measuring Health-State Preferences – I: Measurement Strategies." *Journal of Clinical Epidemiology* 42(4), 345–54.

Froberg, Debra G. (1989*b*) "Methodology for Measuring Health-State Preferences – II: Scaling Methods." *Journal of Clinical Epidemiology* 42(5), 459–71.

——(1989*c*) "Methodology for Measuring Health-State Preferences – III: Population and Context Effects." *Journal of Clinical Epidemiology* 42(6), 585–92.

——(1989*d*) "Methodology for Measuring Health-State Preferences – IV: Progress and a Research Agenda." *Journal of Clinical Epidemiology* 42(7), 675–85.

Gold, Marthe R., Joanna E. Siegel, Louise B. Russell, and Milton C. Weinstein. (1996) *Cost-Effectiveness in Health and Medicine*. New York: Oxford University Press.

Gore, Jr., Al. (1990) "Oregon's Bold Mistake." *Academic Medicine* 65(11), 634–35.

Hadorn, David C. (1991) "Setting Health Care Priorities in Oregon: Cost-Effectiveness Meets the Rule of Rescue." *JAMA* 265(17), 2218–25.

Harris, John. (1985) *The Value of Life*. London: Routledge.

——(1987) "QALYfying the Value of Life." *Journal of Medical Ethics* 13(3), 117–23.

Hausman, Daniel M. (2006) "Valuing Health." *Philosophy and Public Affairs* 34 (3), 246–74.

Hirose, Iwao. (2014*a*) *Egalitarianism*. London: Routledge.

——(2014*b*) *Moral Aggregation*. New York: Oxford University Press.

Jamison, Dean T., Joel G. Breman, Anthony R. Measham, George Alleyne, Mariam Claeson, David B. Evans, Prabhat Jha, Anne Mills, and Philip Musgrove, eds. (2006) *Disease Control Priorities in Developing Countries. 2nd edition*. Washington, DC: Oxford University Press and The World Bank. Also available at http://www.dcp2.org/pubs/DCP.

Johansson, Kjell Arne and Ole Frithjof Norheim. (2011) "Problems With Prioritization: Exploring Ethical Solutions to Inequalities in HIV Care." *The American Journal of Bioethics* 11(12), 32–40.

Kappel, Klemens and Peter Sandøe. (1992) "QALYs, Age and Fairness." *Bioethics* 6(4), 297–316.

Kitzhaber, J. and A. M. Kemmy. (1995) "On the Oregon Trail." *British Medical Bulletin* 51(4), 808–18.

Marmot, Michael. (2004) *The Status Syndrome: How Social Standing Affects Our Health and Longevity*. New York: Henry Holt and Company.

Marmot, M. G., M. J. Shipley, and Geoffrey Rose. (1984) "Inequalities in Death – Specific Explanations of a General Pattern." *The Lancet* 323(8384), 1003–6.

McKerlie, Dennis. (2013) *Justice Between the Young and the Old*. New York: Oxford University Press.

McKie, John, Jeff Richardson, Peter Singer, and Helga Kuhse. (1998) *The Allocation of Health Care Resources: An Ethical Evaluation of the "QALY" Approach*. Aldershot: Ashgate.

Menzel, Paul T. (1990) *Strong Medicine: The Ethical Rationing of Health Care*. New York: Oxford University Press.

Menzel, Paul T., Paul Dolan, Jeff Richardson, and Jan Abel Olsen. (2002) "The Role of Adaptation to Disability and Disease in Health State Valuation: A Preliminary Normative Analysis." *Social Science & Medicine* 55(12), 2149–58.

Murray, Christopher J. L. (1996) "Rethinking DALYs." In Christopher J. L. Murray and Alan D. Lopez (eds.) *The Global Burden of Disease: A Comprehensive Assessment of Mortality and Disability from Diseases, Injuries, and Risk Factors in 1990 and Projected to 2020*, 1–98. Cambridge, MA: Harvard School of Public Health on behalf of the World Health Organization and the World Bank.

Murray, Christopher J. L., Sandeep C. Kulkarni, Catherine Michaud, Niels Tomijima, Maria T. Bulzacchelli, Terrell J. Iandiorio, and Majid Ezzati.

(2006) "Eight Americas: Investigating Mortality Disparities across Races, Counties, and Race-Counties in the United States." *PLoS Medicine* 3(9), 1513–24.

Murray, Christopher J. L., Joshua A. Solomon, Colin D. Mathers and Alan D. Lopez, eds. (2002) *Summary Measures of Population Health: Concepts, Ethics, Measurement and Applications*. Geneva: World Health Organization.

Nagel, Thomas. (1979) "Equality." In *Mortal Questions*, 106–27. New York: Cambridge University Press.

Nord, Erik. (1993) "The Trade-Off between Severity of Illness and Treatment Effect in Cost-Value Analysis of Health Care." *Health Policy* 24(3), 227–38.

——(1999) *Cost-Value Analysis in Health Care: Making Sense Out of QALYs*. Cambridge: Cambridge University Press.

Nord, Erik, Norman Daniels, and Mark Kamlet. (2009) "QALYs: Some Challenges." *Value in Health* 12(suppl. 1), S10–S15.

Nord, Erik, Jose Luis Pinto, Jeff Richardson, Paul Menzel, and Peter Ubel. (1999) "Incorporating Societal Concerns for Fairness in Numerical Valuations of Health Programs." *Health Economics* 8(1), 25–39.

Olsen, Jan Abel, Jeff Richardson, Paul Dolan, and Paul Menzel. (2003) "The Moral Relevance of Personal Characteristics in Setting Health Care Priorities." *Social Science & Medicine* 57(7), 1163–72.

Parfit, Derek. (1995) "Equality or Priority?" The Lindley Lecture, 1991. Department of Philosophy, University of Kansas. Reprinted in Matthew Clayton and Andrew Williams (eds.) *The Ideal of Equality*, 81–125. Basingstoke: Palgrave, 2002.

Peterson, Martin. (2008) "The Moral Importance of Selecting People Randomly." *Bioethics* 22(6), 321–27.

Phillips, David. (2006) *Quality of Life: Concept, Policy and Practice*. New York: Routledge.

Rawlins, Michael D. and Anthony J. Culyer. (2004) "National Institute for Clinical Excellence and Its Value Judgments." *British Medical Journal* 329, 224–27.

Roemer, John E. (1993) "A Pragmatic Theory of Responsibility for the Egalitarian Planner." *Philosophy and Public Affairs* 22(2), 146–66.

Scanlon, Thomas M. (1998) *What We Owe to Each Other*. Cambridge, MA: Harvard Unviversity Press.

Segall, Shlomi. (2010) *Health, Luck and Justice*. Princeton, NJ: Princeton University Press.

Shah, Koonal K. (2009) "Severity of Illness and Priority Setting in Healthcare: A Review of the Literature." *Health Policy* 93(2–3), 77–84.

Singer, Peter, John McKie, Helga Kuhse, and Jeff Richardson. (1995) "Double Jeopardy and the Use of QALYs in Health Care Allocation." *Journal of Medical Ethics* 21(3), 144–50.

Taurek, John. (1977) "Should the Numbers Count?" *Philosophy and Public Affairs* 6(4), 293–316.

Timmons, Mark. (2013) *Moral Theory: An Introduction*. 2nd edition. Lanham, MD: Rowman & Littlefield.

Tooley, Michael. (1972) "Abortion and Infanticide." *Philosophy and Public Affairs* 2(1), 37–65.

Tungodden, Bertil. (2003) "The Value of Equality." *Economics and Philosophy* 19(1), 1–44.

Ubel, Peter A. (2000) *Pricing Life: Why It's Time for Health Care Rationing*. Cambridge, MA: The MIT Press.

Ubel, Peter A., Jonathan Baron, and David A. Asch. (1999) "Social Responsibility, Personal Responsibility, and Prognosis in Public Judgments about Transplant Allocation." *Bioethics* 13(1), 57–68.

Ubel, Peter A., Michael L. DeKay, Jonathan Baron, and David A. Asch. (1996) "Cost-Effectiveness Analysis in a Setting of Budget Constraints: Is It Equitable?" *The New England Journal of Medicine* 334(18), 1174–77.

UNDP. (2011) *Sustainability and Equity: A Better Future for All. Human Development Report 2011*. New York: Palgrave Macmillan for the United Nations Development Programme.

Verweij, Marcel. (2009) "Moral Principles for Allocating Scarce Medical Resources in an Influenza Pandemic." *Journal of Bioethical Inquiry* 6(2), 159–69.

Wagstaff, Adam. (1991) "QALYs and the Equity-Efficiency Trade-Off." *Journal of Health Economics* 10(1), 21–41.

Weinstein, Milton C., George Torrance, and Alistair McGuire. (2009) "QALYs: The Basics." *Value in Health* 12(suppl. 1), S5–S9.

WHO. (2010) *Health Systems Financing: The Path to Universal Coverage. World Health Report 2010*. Geneva: World Health Organization.

Wikler, Daniel. (2004) "Personal and Social Responsibility for Health." In Anand *et al.* (2004), 109–34.

Wilkinson, Stephen. (1999) "Smokers' Rights to Health Care: Why the 'Restoration Argument' is a Moralising Wolf in a Liberal Sheep's Clothing." *Journal of Applied Philosophy* 16(3), 255–69.

Williams, Alan. (1997) "Intergenerational Equity: An Exploration of the 'Fair Innings' Argument." *Health Economics* 6(2), 117–32.

Wolff, Jonathan, Sarah Edwards, Sarah Richmond, Shepley Orr, and Geraint Rees. (2012) "Evaluating Interventions in Health: A Reconciliatory Approach." *Bioethics* 26(9), 455–63.

Index

"3 by 5" program 10–11, 16

abandonment objection 132, 141;
  pluralist response to 132–3
abortion 3, 19–20
access to health care 16, 63, 149,
  155–6; equal 144
Acheson report 145
adaptation 50–1
age: discrimination by *see* ageism;
  weighted DALY 96–9, 168;
  weighted QALY 120, 150;
  weighting 95–6, 158; weighting
  function 96–98, 120
ageism: prioritarian 120; utilitarian
  89–95, 120
aggregation: problem 106, 111–12,
  158; thesis 106, 111, 117–18, 155,
  158
alcohol 44, 59, 118, 135, 138; and
  excess drinking 128–9, 139; -related
  health problem 118; taxation on 59,
  135, 138
Americans with Disabilities Act 61,
  80, 143
antenatal screening 118
antiretroviral therapy 10–11, 16,
  46–7
axiological concepts 24

Blair, T. 149
bottomless pit problem 87, 123

brute luck 129; and luck
  egalitarianism 131–2

cancer 46, 129; breast 133, 141; colon
  77; drugs 3, 63; liver 76; lung 47,
  149; patients 43; screening 13, 17;
  terminal 18, 64, 87, 88; treatment
  58, 133
causal relation 145–6
chronic health condition *see* disability
class *see* socioeconomic group
co-payment 3, 13, 65, 136, 139, 140
condition-treatment pairs 61, 82, 104
consequentialism 24–5, 158
cost-effectiveness analysis 4–5, 158;
  and DALY 58–9, 66, 75, 95, 98–9;
  and equity weights 70–4, 154; and
  QALY 57–9, 62, 65–7, 72–84, 89,
  98, 106
cost-effectiveness ratio 54, 55, 79,
  121; and DALY 66; and NICE 64,
  75; and QALY 73, 76, 80, 84, 89

DALY 44–9, 57–9, 62, 79, 158; and
  age-weighting 95–9; and the
  aggregation thesis 106; and the
  and discounting 75–7; Disease
  Control Priorities Project 65–6
deontology 24–5, 158
disability: -adjusted life year *see*
  DALY; discrimination objection
  80–1, 99, 154, 158

disability weights 46–8, 58–9, 95; in
　Disease Control Priorities Project
　66; and PHARMAC 62
discounting 39–40, 74–7
discrimination: against the old *see*
　ageism; against patients with
　disabilities 80–4, 86, 88
Disease Control Priorities Project
　65–6, 75, 98

education 17, 41; and health inequalities
　127, 139, 142–4, 146, 148
efficiency 73, 74, 153
egalitarianism 120–1, 158; leveling
　down objection to 120–1, 130, 158;
　luck *see* luck egalitarianism
EQ-5D 33–4, 49, 62, 158;
　questionnaire of 34
equal access view 144, 159
equity: -efficiency trade offs
　73–4; -weighted QALY 106, 119–20;
　weights 70–4, 94, 99, 119, 154
ethics 19; and burden of proof 23–4;
　and consistency 23; and intuitions
　21–3; and law 20, and
　relativism 20–1

fair chance 100, 112–14, 159
fair equality of opportunity view
　137–9, 144, 159
fair innings argument 89, 159;
　argument for 89–93; and DALY 96;
　objections to 93–4; and the
　significance of age 94–5
free will 140–1

GDP 15, 40–1, 156
gender 100, 127, 138
Global Burden of Disease studies
　44–8, 62, 66, 75, 77, 95–8
God committee 27
Gore, A. 61

HALE 42–3, 63, 68–9, 159
health; -adjusted life expectancy *see*
　HALE; inequality and
　socioeconomic status *see* social
　gradient of health; and
　inseparability problem 32–3,
　50; -only framework 127–8, 146,
　148; value of 30–1; and well-being
　29–33, 41–2, 50, 77, 81, 85, 97,
　124, 152–3; WHO definition
　of 31
health benefit: aggregation of 104–6;
　calculation of overall 57–9;
　discounting the future 74–7;
　measure of 55; and NICE 64–5; and
　PHARMAC 62–3; utilitarian
　distribution of 65–6, 71–3
health insurance 15, 26, 77, 88;
　package 29, 54; private 4, 11, 102
Herceptin 63–4, 82
HIV/AIDS 33, 44, 47–8, 61
human capital argument 97
Human Development Index 41

incremental cost-effectiveness 55, 64
inequality: equity weights for
　reducing 72, 99; health 16, 67–9,
　129–31, 144–6; income 16, 143–8;
　in life chances 68; lifetime 68;
　socioeconomic 69, 144–6
infanticide 22–3
intuitions 21; and the aggregation of
　health benefits 107–8; conflict of
　22–3; and responsibility in
　health 129–33, 140; and the
　significance of age 95

justice 41, 100, 129–33, 145–8

leveling down objection 120–1, 130,
　159
leximin 122–3, 159

life expectancy 41, 44, 46, 58, 156;
  health-adjusted *see* HALE
lottery: by coin-toss 109–10; and
  maximal chance 115; postcode *see*
  postcode lottery; weighted 113–17;
  see also fair chances
luck egalitarianism 129, 159;
  abandonment objection to 132,
  141; all- 137, 144
luck prioritarianism 131

maximin 122, 159
maximization: benefit 10, 24, 73, 89,
  90, 106, 107, 113, 117, 119, 154; of
  health benefits 25, 67, 98, 101, 106
Medicaid 60–1, 78, 82, 83, 104
Medicare 85
mobility 34–6, 81
morbidity 59, 95–8, 143–6
mortality: and DALY 44–7, 95–8;
  gap 67–8, 142–6; and public health
  117

NHS 63, 121, 143
NICE 64–6, 73, 82, 104, 153;
  Citizen Councils of 65
number problem 108–10, 159

obesity 128, 135, 139; and bariatric
  surgery 149
OECD 15, 156
option luck 129; and luck
  egalitarianism 131–2
Oregon: Health Plan 60–2, 66, 82,
  85, 104–5; Medicaid reform 60–1,
  82, 104
organ transplantation 12, 29

pairwise comparison: of health states
  49; principle of 107–9, 160
pandemic flu 3, 12, 117
pharmaceuticals 3, 12–13, 62–3, 66,
  82, 104, 152

PHRMAC 62–3, 66, 73
population-level bioethics 3, 154
postcode lottery 63–4, 68
prevention paradox 118
prioritarianism 72, 119, 130–1, 155,
  160; and the aggregation problem
  122; and the bottomless pit
  problem 123; and egalitarianism 120;
  and leximin 122; QALY 120, 124
priority list 54, 99, 111; Oregon's
  60–2, 70, 84–5, 88, 104
priority setting 1, 3, 65, 138, 154,
pure time preferences 75–6, 160

QALY 4, 43, 160; age-weighted 106,
  120; aggregation of 90, 106,
  119–20, 124; equity-weighted
  106; and individuals with
  disabilities 80–4; and NICE 64–5,
  66, 73, 82; and the old 89;
  and Oregon 61–2, 66, 82, 84, 105;
  and PHARMAC 62, 64, 66, 73,
  82; prioritarianism 72, 119, 124;
  and utilitarianism 66–7, 72, 106

rating scale method 35–6, 38–40, 160
rationing: bedside 151–2; inevitability
  of 2, 14, 18, 152; and scarcity 4,
  12, 14, 16–18, 31, 83, 148,
  151–2, 155–6; ubiquity of 10
relativism 20–1
rescue case 108–9, 112–16, 154
responsibility 129, 133, 135, 136,
  147; and all-luck egalitarianism
  137; irrelevance of 135, 138,
  139, 155; and luck egalitarianism
  129, 130, 131, 134; of
  policymakers 11; pragmatic
  notion of 141; and priority setting
  138, 139; and risk factors 128; and
  socioeconomic status 140–1
rights 18, 24, 25; to health care 18;
  human 82; women's 100

risk: attitude 39, 40; factor 43, 65,
    128, 143; health 57, 114

schizophrenia 44, 47
sequelae 46
severity of illness 65, 69, 73, 87
sexual orientation 82, 127
smoking 128–9, 134–5, 138–9, 143,
    149; anti- 59
social determinants of health 6, 141,
    144–8, 160
social gradient in health 141, 144–6, 160
socioeconomic group 41, 43, 65, 67–9,
    146
Socrates 157
standard gamble 37–40, 160
strictly concave function 119–20, 126;
    see also prioritarianism

tie breaking argument 110
time trade-off 38–40
top up 64–5, 121, 154
triage 83, 116, 160
triple jeopardy 140

UNAIDS 10
unfair: discrimination against people
    with disabilities 74, 79, 80, 86, 88,
    99, 102; treatment 102; *see also* fair

United Cerebral Palsy Associations
    61, 82
utilitarianism 66–7, 72, 106, 160

vaccination 7–12, 16, 21, 24, 28,
    100, 143; and influenza pandemic
    3, 117
value: absolute 112; comparison of 52;
    of health 31, 32, 40; instrumental
    31; intrinsic 31; for monetary 55,
    56; money 31, 54, 62, 98, 104,
    148; moral 71–3, 94, 120, 126n;
    present 75; relative 37, 70, 96;
    summary 33, 44

waiting list 1, 3, 12, 29, 102, 114,
    124–5
welfare interdependence 97
well-being: component of 31, 32, 42,
    50, 79, 81, 120; and health 29–33,
    41–2, 50, 77, 81, 85, 97, 124,
    152–3; impact on 33, 79; overall
    32, 50, 85, 97, 120, 124
Whitehall studies 142–3
WHO 31, 44, 63, 65; Commission on
    Social Determinants of Health of
    145, 149–50

CPSIA information can be obtained at www.ICGtesting.com
Printed in the USA
BVOW01s0016200215

388534BV00003B/26/P